April 1

Dear Gerry.

Hot off the presses!

With best wishes,

Jim

A Piece
of Valiant Dust

An Essay in Living

J. A. Hijiya

A Piece of Valiant Dust

Library of Congress Control Number: 2017902046

CreateSpace Independent Publishing Platform,
North Charleston, SC

A Piece of Valiant Dust

For Henry Hideo Fukai

"Uncle Hank"

You can attach the whole of moral philosophy to a commonplace private life as well as to one of richer stuff. Every man bears the whole Form of the human condition.

To enjoy life requires some husbandry. I enjoy it twice as much as others, since the measure of our joy depends on the greater or lesser degree of our attachment to it . . . Others know the delight of happiness and well-being: I know it as they do, but not *en passant*, as it slips by. We must also study it, savour it, muse upon it . . . .

Life must be its own objective, its own purpose. Its right concern is to rule itself, govern itself, put up with itself. Numbered among its other duties included under the general and principal heading, *How to live*, there is the sub-section, *How to die*.

Montaigne, *Essays*, Book III
M. A. Screech, trans.

A Piece of Valiant Dust

Contents

❋ Acknowledgments ❋

Memory Lane may look like a well-traveled road; but it is, in fact, the most tenuous of trails, fast overgrown by the weeds of time. Family members and old friends have rescued me when I was lost: telling me what I didn't know, reminding me of what I had forgotten, and correcting me when I remembered what had never actually occurred. For such assistance, then, I thank Namiko Hijiya, Robert Hijiya, Janice Hijiya Price, Richard O'Leary, and the late Henry Fukai.

Three people read the entire manuscript and wrote detailed criticisms and suggestions for every chapter and practically every page. For such generosity I am grateful to James Marlow, the late Michael Kammen, and the late John Werly. Dr. Marlow also encouraged me to publish this book independently and provided me with invaluable assistance in the process of production. Many other people critiqued a part of the manuscript, responded to a question or comment from me, or, learning of my project, offered useful advice and encouragement. For all this assistance I thank Thomas Ager, Christina Ager, Shaleen

A Piece of Valiant Dust

Barnes, Jessica Bram, Nurit Budinsky, Eleanor Carlson, Jennifer Wong Chacón, Michael Cortese, Thomas Goin, David Heyamoto, the late Fumiko Heyamoto, Richard Hogan, Carol Kammen, Clark Larsen, the late Sachiko Maeda, Corinne Marlow, the late Robert Michael, Betty Mitchell, the late Edward Szymanoski, Stephen Wasby, Robert Waxler, Bonnie Werly, J. B. Whitney, and Susan Whitney. Richard Legault guided me out of box canyons in the unforgiving terrain of Microsoft Word. I also thank Darcie Brand for the use of an oral history of her grandmother, Sachi Maeda, that Darcie recorded in 1996. The fact that so many of these people are listed as "the late" suggests how woefully long it has taken me to publish this book.

Last but the very opposite of least, I thank my wife, Barbara Najjar. She urged me to write the book, she read the manuscript in several versions, and she commented on it helpfully. She also assisted in a very material way by paying the bills after I quit my job so I could spend more time writing. Her appearance in the Epilogue brings this book to a close; but in real life, she's the one who made it possible to get it started.

Doubtless, there are people whose assistance I have forgotten to mention. To such people I offer no excuses, only apologies.

Under the title "Japanese American Dilemmas," Chapter Three of this book appeared in *Antioch Review*, vol. 66, no. 2 (Spring 2008). The Epilogue, "Numbers," appeared in *Raritan*, vol. 32, no. 4 (Spring 2013). Chapter

A Piece of Valiant Dust

Nine appeared in the Spring/Summer 2017 issue of *Two Hawks Quarterly* under the title "Ah-DAH! A Literary Education." I thank the editors of these journals for bringing those essays into daylight and now allowing them, slightly modified, to be seen again.

The illustration on the right side of the cover is a scanning electron micrograph of house dust, taken by Dennis Kunkel Microscopy/Science Source and reproduced by permission. The photo shows dog hair (dark brown), cat hair (orange), plant fibers (green), other fibers (purple, pink, blue), spider silk (turquoise), and dirt and dead skin (brown). The skin could be the author's but isn't. The cover was designed by Daniel Tetrault of CreateSpace.

The Montaigne epigraphs come from *The Complete Essays*, trans. M. A. Screech (New York: Penguin, 1991).

A Piece of Valiant Dust is dedicated to the memory of Henry Hideo Fukai (1923-2012), known as Uncle Hank even to people to whom he was not technically related. He was endlessly generous, thoughtful, and kind. Everyone should have such an uncle.

South Dartmouth, Massachusetts
February 2017

Prologue

❄ Names ❄

all me Hijiya.

HEE-JEE-YAH, rhyming with nothing. You have called me by other names.

Hy-JEE-uh: Hygeia, Greek goddess of health, a fitting idol for a man of my infirmities. "Get the right idea, vote for Jim Hijiya!"—my campaign slogan for Student Council president in eighth grade. It did not prevent my election.

Hih-JEE-uh, with a short *i* in the first syllable and, inconsistently, a long *e* in the second. My most common appellation—what most of my friends call me, and what I usually call myself.

Hih-ZHEE-uh: the sexy, frenched pronunciation preferred by my friend Betty.

Just plain HIDGE, rhyming with fridge. What they call me at restaurants, because that's all I tell them when I make a reservation. If I give my whole name, then no matter how slowly I spell it, how precisely I enunciate each letter, they ask me to repeat it, often twice, then they spell it "Hijaya" and can't pronounce it at all. So I just say, "Hij: H-I-J, three consecutive letters in the alphabet, yes that's it, easy as pie, may I please have a table for two at seven?"

When I wrote for the high school newspaper, my by-line was Hij. The first time my mother saw that name in print, she was startled. She told me Hij had been my *father's* nickname. I look very much like him in an old brown photo in which he is cleaning a pistol. I don't remember ever seeing him in person, though I suppose that he saw me.

In college I asked a professor of Asian religions what "Hijiya" meant. He said he couldn't tell for sure unless he saw it written in Japanese; but I didn't know how to do that, how to write my own name. He said it might mean "House of the Rising Sun." Then again, he said, it might mean "House at the Foot of the Hill."

?

!

Am I allowed to choose the house into which I am born?

When I was small, I knew a girl who had heard me called "Jimmy" or, more formally, "Jim Hijiya," so she thought my name was Jimmy Jiya. Her name was Kiyomi, pronounced Kee-YO-mee. I heard it differently, however, so I called her "Kill Me." Even though we were both Japanese, we could make no sense of Japanese names like Hijiya or Kiyomi, so we unwittingly translated them into something we could understand, something American.

The name of my mother's family is Fukai, the first syllable pronounced with an emphatically long *u*: FOO! My mother's parents emigrated from Okayama Prefecture, right next to Hiroshima. John Hersey's famous book about the atomic bombing tells of a Mr. Fukai who at first

2

fled the burning city but then, seeing what had become of his world, turned around and ran directly into the flames. Like many Japanese, Mr. Fukai was an idealist.

I have been told that in Japan the Fukais were samurai. I have been told the same about the Hijiyas, though I also have been told that they were farmers. I suspect that most Japanese Americans have heard they are descended from the aristocratic warrior class. Once in a while, it may even be true. In the late nineteenth and early twentieth centuries, when the Japanese were migrating to America, there wasn't much work left in Japan for swordsmen. These people had education, ambition, and enough money to buy passage to America, so some of them did. Whether any of them were named Fukai or Hijiya, however, I do not know. I suppose I could do genealogical research to find out, but, frankly, I don't see what difference it would make. Even if all my ancestors were samurai, I would still be me.

Most of my friends call me "Jim," though my college buddies say "J. A." Some people who knew me as a kid still call me "Jimmy." So do a few close friends I've met more recently. I don't like it, though, when the diminutive is applied by strangers. White men, mostly.

The first name on my birth certificate is James—derived from the Hebrew *Jacob*, the Supplanter. I guess Jacob was actually a Usurper, having stolen his brother Esau's birthright. I am my parents' second son, and my brother still complains that I got special treatment. I started collecting an allowance at age five, while he and my sister had had to wait until they were six. Maybe it was because I was the last-born, the "baby of the family," or maybe because I had had polio. Jacob hurt his leg by wrestling with an angel; I, with infantile paralysis. When I was a child, my mother would cradle my right foot in her lap each night, her palm on my sole, pressing the foot upward as I willed to press it down, trying to bring dead muscles back to life. Wiggle my big toe? You might as well ask me to fly. For me, exercise has always been a hopeless prayer.

Although Jacob got to keep what he had stolen, he never ceased to pay for it. His son Joseph, his youngest and favorite child, got sold into slavery by resentful older brothers—retribution for their father's habitual overturning of familial order. Jacob didn't have an easy life. But, then, who does?

I live today in a village called Padanaram (Paid-uh-NAIR-um), same as the plain in the Valley of the Euphrates, land of the Patriarchs, where Jacob sojourned to find a wife. Our village was named by a man named Laban, like the father of Leah and Rachel, who became Jacob's first and second wives. It was in Johnstown, Pennsylvania, that I met Barbara, the woman who would become my wife, but I was living in Padanaram at the time.

I have no children. If I am a Jacob, it is a barren one, the end of the line, very unlike the one in the Bible. That's the trouble with archetypes: you can never live up to them. That does not mean, however, that they don't exist.

My middle name, Alan, means nothing. My mother says she just liked the sound of it. For that same reason she gave my brother the middle name Owen. He got his first name, Robert, from Uncle Bob, my mother's oldest brother, who became head of the family when my mother was orphaned at the age of twelve. So even though my brother was named Robert Owen, his nomenclature did no honor to the British utopian social reformer of whom no one in the family had ever heard. My brother is a conservative.

My sister, Janice, got her first name from the singing movie actress Janis Paige. However, Mom changed the spelling from N-I-S to N-I-C-E because she wanted her daughter to be "nice." But Janice didn't start out that way. My mother tells this story of my sister's birth:

"Bear down, Mrs. Hijiya."

"Unh."

"Bear down!"

"UNNNHHHH!"

(   )

"Who prepared this woman? Wasn't she given an enema?"

As Saint Augustine pointed out, we are born between feces and urine. That's true of everybody, but especially my sister.

Mom says that Bob's birth was long and painful, Janice's less so, and mine as easy as a bowel movement. Maybe that was why she gave me my allowance early.

But wasn't I talking about names?

My father was called George because that was one of the few American names his parents knew. George

5

Washington. George Jessel. "By George!" "Let George do it." There were many Georges among the first two generations of Japanese in America. My mother's father was named Keiichi (meaning "respectful first son"), with a double-i that made it hard for white people to spell or pronounce or conceptualize, so they called him "George." That simple moniker also belonged to my Aunt Fumi's husband. So my mother had a father, a husband, and a brother-in-law all named George.

George was not the only name possible for a Japanese man. There also was Frank. My father's father was named Kohei, but white people called him Frank. His daughter Sachiko married a man named Frank. Among Japanese men, American names were in short supply, so they had to be shared.

Japanese women weren't given American names at all, apparently because they were not expected to be needed. What reason would a Japanese woman ever have to tell her personal name to whites? Wouldn't "Miss" or "Mrs." always suffice? My father's mother was Masuae; her daughters were Sachiko and Terue. My mother's mother was Katano; her daughters were Tomiko, Fumiko, and Namiko.

Men of my father's generation had a Japanese middle name after their American first name. For my father it was Yukio, like the personal name of Yukio Mishima, author of the novel *Spring Snow*—*yuki* means "snow." "George Yukio Hijiya" is what it says on the stiff, white-on-black photostatic copy of the papers discharging him from the army.

He earned two Bronze Stars and a Purple Heart but left the army at the rank of private. My file-clerk uncles, Mason and Hank, made sergeant; but my father, a rifleman who fought the Germans from Rome to the Rhineland, outlasting half the men (or so it seemed) in the 442nd Regimental Combat Team, a unit with so many casualties that enlisted men regularly got battlefield promotions to the officer class—my father, I repeat, never even made corporal. I never learned why. It was an evil omen.

My mother doesn't know why she was named Namiko, but *nami* means wave. You have heard of a tsunami, a tidal wave which, like all other tidal waves, has nothing to do with the tide. Her high school history teacher called her Nakimo (nuh-KIM-oh), so we children of hers jestingly call her that. This is what happens to you when you're born in a foreign country.

I was born on the third of August 1949, a Wednesday. If you remember a certain nursery rhyme, you may believe that I am a "Wednesday's child," born to woe. What truth is there in poetry?

See me as I am:

My hair is dry and curly; no longer black, but not yet perfectly white; a patchwork of pale gray; a great ball of dingy cotton if I let it grow long. In my youth I invented the Jafro, but now I ask the stylist to cut my hair as short as scissors can. I refuse the electric clippers because I prefer something slower, the touch of a woman's hand. My scalp is not a lawn.

I wear titanium-rimmed spectacles with thick lenses that distort. My left eye is lower on my face and squintier than my right, just as my left ear is lower than my right. My head is, as they say in the South, half a bubble off plumb. My nose is flat, my teeth white but uneven, my throat splotched red with chronic eczema. My shoulders are narrow, and my chest is flat and hairless. My biceps make no bulge, and my fingers are such stubs that single-handed and palm down, I cannot hold onto a football. My belly is the Laughing Buddha's, a protuberant one you would rub for good luck, but I wear loose shirts and baggy sweaters to conceal it. My hips and thighs are padded with fat like a woman's.

I am not attractive. Once I rode in an elevator with a young girl and her mother—just the three of us in a cozy compartment for a ride to the heights. The child stared up at me, and I smiled down at her. As I stepped out, I heard her exclaim to her mother, "What an ugly man!" The doors clanked shut before I could reach back and strangle the babe. In fairness to her, however, I should say that she was observant, as children often are, even if indiscreet.

I am five feet six inches tall when I stand with my weight on my left leg, five feet five on my right. I walk with a limp. My gait is the letter A in Morse Code (dih-daah), the left foot dashing the right foot's dot. When I go downtown, I observe my reflection in storefront windows: the tiny jerk of my whole body as the sturdy left foot jumps forward suddenly to relieve the weight, sometimes the pain, from the enfeebled right.

Names

I take interest in my deformity, as do others. Sometimes as I pass through a crowd, men and women, out of boredom, let their eyes slide sideways and poke me for a moment, then slide back to their proper fixture. Children take me in, in one quick uninhibited stare: cripple. But no stranger speaks to me of my infirmity.

Perhaps I think of it too much, perhaps I am obsessed. If I put away my microscope of consciousness—my favorite toy!—I find my limp less spectacular than I had imagined. Some acquaintances long fail to notice it, and when at last they do, they ask if I have hurt myself. I tell them yes, I've been going to and fro in the earth, and my leg is tired. A little lie saves a long story. Or sometimes they ask what's wrong with my leg, thinking that perhaps I have sprained an ankle, but I say, "Polio," and enjoy their embarrassment. What can they do but stammer apologies?

But you, my friends, will know better. To you I shall anatomize myself, part by ungainly part, until the strange becomes familiar. Yet it will not be me you know but only fragments of me: my foot, my skin, my eyes, my mouth. These organs are mine but could just as well be yours. Have you no eyes? No feet? If I tickle you, will you not laugh? In the funhouse mirror that is me, you may detect a reflection of yourself. What you see there, however, you may never have noticed before.

I shall speak of myself but not of my self; not of my life but of living. What I offer you is not biography, the story of a man, but anthropology, the study of humankind. I am no meticulous autobiographer, marching you past the obligatory landmarks of my particular little life—parents, birth, schooling, employment, achievements, wife—all in tidy chronological order, with dates and place names cementing every event into position. No, not at all. If you learn any of that about me, it will be only by accident, not because I have made a point of telling you. And why should I? I am no eminent personage, no subject of an article in *Who's Who* or Wikipedia, whose parade through history you wish to observe. I am nobody, a clown singing at the moon.

Perhaps, however, you will recognize the song.

I have many stories to tell you but no story. If you go looking for a "narrative arc," a rainbow landing in a dramaturgical pot of gold, you will be disappointed. There is no development here: no action, no climax, and surely no resolution. Shakespeare I am not. Even when I follow chronology—first this, then that—there is no dynamic connection between events, no causation. What I have to tell you seems less like biography than physiology, less like a portrait than a gallery of still lifes—brazen examples of that humblest and most detested of genres—relentless observations of mere things. I might as well be painting pictures of cabbages and quinces.

But that's because I'm talking about me. My life does not have the makings of a story, or at least it will not until I am dead. How can you have a beginning and a middle when you don't have an end? There is very little change in my life: it's a chronic condition. So my narrative doesn't go anywhere. It's already there. If you want to find

10

structure in my life, you will have to search its pieces for a pattern, not a plot. Do I repeat myself? Very well then I repeat myself. (I am small, I contain redundancies.)

Charles Wright is right:

> Ah, description, of all the arts the least
>   appreciated.
> Well, it's just this and it's just that,
>   someone will point out.
> Exactly.   It's just this and it's just that and
>   nothing other.

But will you stay with me and investigate a life in which nothing happens, the natural history of a piece of valiant dust? Or will you slink back and, while I am raving, wordlessly depart, grateful to escape much ado about nothing?

Quite possibly. To you I say fare well. May you find happiness in the drama of events. But to those patient souls who prefer the microscope to the motion picture, I have something to show. Here, behind the curtain.

Chapter One

❊ My Right Foot ❊

My mind got off on the right foot. Yes, my shrunken, misshapen, feeble right foot—this was what got me thinking. Dostoevsky says that suffering is the sole origin of consciousness. For me, though, it was not suffering—nothing that dramatic—but only discomfort, inconvenience, and embarrassment.

When I was a child, the squeak of my brace sometimes made passers-by glance at me. If I had gone too many days without squeezing fat yellow drops of Three-in-One Oil into the ankle joints of the brace, it would proclaim the effects of constant friction and occasional rain. The rhythmic squeal of metal on metal at every other step would tell the world of my approach.

I had a half-leg brace: shiny, flattened, steel shafts erupting from each side of the heel of my right shoe, ascending two inches before dissolving into circular joints at the ankle, then re-emerging and climbing again to disappear finally into a perpendicular swath of padded brown leather that wrapped my calf, cinched tight by a buckle with two steel prongs. The harness chafed the skin, drawing blood, staining the leather with a ragged dark splotch that sometimes resembled a peanut and sometimes Australia.

It was the brace—the animal hide and stainless steel that enabled me to walk—that made me aware that my body was, like the brace itself, a machine; a gravely defective machine, to be sure, but one whose parts could be repaired or replaced. My foot was something strange: not just odd but alien, a foreign object like a block of wood attached to the bottom of my leg. The brace, giving rigor to my right foot, taught me that my body was a *thing*, an object for me to observe, manipulate, enjoy, resent, and fear. My body was not me. As a child, I did not ask *who* I was but *what*.

The question arose shortly after I began to walk. As my mother paraded me around the neighborhood, our next-door neighbor noticed something wrong with my gait: a lurch, a stumbling. My mother took me to a doctor who said I had had polio. Past perfect tense—*had* had: maybe in the first weeks of life, maybe even in the womb (my mother had gotten very sick, bedridden, while pregnant with me). By the time the disease was diagnosed, however, it was gone. Mia Farrow, the actor, says that when she contracted polio at the age of nine, her childhood ended. If the disease had had the same effect on me, I would have had no childhood at all.

Though I didn't know it at the time, I had taken part in an epidemic. In 1949, the year I contracted polio, there were 42,000 cases reported in the United States—by far the largest number in any year to that point, though it would soon be exceeded. The victims were mostly children and mostly boys, like myself. The nation feared and battled polio as if it were communism. Newspapers warned of the disease's spread, and magazines published photographs of children in iron lungs. Women by the thousands went door to door, collecting money for the March of Dimes, which funded research on the disease. (Since 1946, the ten-cent piece had featured a profile of Franklin Roosevelt, polio's most prominent victim.) By 1955, Jonas Salk's vaccine was being injected into the arms of millions of grimacing children.

This was too late for me, however. At the end of my right leg, my foot already dangled uselessly, an obtuse angle of broken meat. When I tried to walk, the foot did not obey the brain, following instead no law but gravity. Drop foot, the doctors called it. The appendage sloped down, dead toes banging into dead earth. The virus had infiltrated my spinal cord and murdered the nerves activating the muscles of my foot. The nerves that registered pain, however, remained very much alive; and they screamed each time I stubbed my naked toes.

The brace changed all that. The brace, my own personal *deus ex machina*, raised my foot like Lazarus, so that instead of drooping, it projected properly perpendicular to the shin as I strode forward. Now my lower extremity from calf to toe was armored into a perpetual L. Now I could walk, even run.

Not that I became fleet. I was always the slowest boy in the neighborhood. Even Little Larry (so called because there was another, much larger Larry living a block away), two years younger than me, could beat me in a race. Once during a softball game, as I lugged my body down the first-base line, one of my friends said it looked as if I were running underwater.

I went through childhood with one pair of shoes—one at any given time, that is. They were brown high-tops, supporting my ankles by covering them with leather, and for me they were always in fashion. With only one brace and with that brace permanently attached to one right shoe, I always had to use that shoe. My brother and sister had choices: black shoes as well as brown, shiny ones for church, white sneakers or even red ones for playing softball in the street, rubber sandals in colors gaudy or subdued. But I had a single pair of shoes. When I outgrew them or wore them out, I would get another pair just like them: Shoes Universal, for all times, everywhere.

This made me conspicuous at school. In PE class all the other boys wore tennis shoes; not me. In weekly square-dancing class the other children do-si-doed silently in stockinged feet, while my leather-soled clodhoppers squeaked on the wooden floor and imperiled the toes of my assigned partner, whose only defense was distance—a defense she scrupulously maintained. My shoes left dull black scuff marks on the floor of the gym.

I could not wear *zori*, nowadays called flip-flops, the sandals with a fat rubber thong between the big toe and the next, because to keep them on while you walk, your toes need to press up on the V-shaped strap above the thong or down on the sole, a task my toes could not perform. The sandal would fall off.

I could walk barefoot alongside a swimming pool, but I could not run. If I tried, the big toe would curl under the ball of my foot and grind against the hot, rough cement, crushing little joints in explosions of pain as I went sprawling. So instead I walked slowly and deliberately, choreographing each step, lifting the knee, swinging the foot forward, trying to lay it down flat.

It was easier to wear the brace. I strapped it on as soon as I left the swimming pool. I wore it on the bus going home. I wore it around the house. I wore it to school. I wore it when I helped my brother on his paper route. I wore it to church. I wore it when I played softball. Sometimes I even wore it to bed, wrapped in a pillowcase so my shoe wouldn't soil the sheets. The brace, the brace, always the brace.

But no! Not always, not forever. I threw it away and walked unaided after going to the Shrine.

Perhaps you think I am about to tell you of a miracle, of wonder-working faith. If so, however, you don't know me at all. No, my foot's transfiguration was nothing so histrionic and sublime. It was more like a trip to the body shop.

When I was twelve, the doctors said I was old enough, my bones now hardened sufficiently, my body approximating its adult dimensions, for me to have corrective surgery. A "triple arthrodesis," a fusing of bones in the ankle—an operation that has been called the "surgical obliteration" of a joint—*this* would fix my foot permanently and inflexibly in the shape of an L, the soldered bones reclaiming their original organizing function and supplanting my grotesque exoskeleton of leather and steel. My foot would at last be free.

I left school in December and spent Christmas Day opening presents at the Shrine—Shriners Hospital for Crippled Children, that is, but everybody called it the Shrine. On the day after Christmas, a Tuesday, I went under the knife. At the Shrine, surgeries were always performed on Tuesday, investing that day with a special excitement. As I lay on my back and the nurses wheeled me out of my ward on a gurney, the other boys lined up along my path and gave words to Chopin's funeral march: "Pray . . . for . . . the dead, . . . and . . . the dead . . . will pray . . . for you . . . ." On later Tuesdays I would add my voice to this dirge for boys about to be carved.

When I woke up, I found that my right leg had been turned into a piece of statuary, a thick white shell from crotch to toes, a crude plaster copy of a leg, bent obliquely at the knee. This I would carry for the next two months.

Something there is that does not love the whiteness of a cast. The bright blankness stares at you and demands violation. Autographs, doodles, black ink laid down like a challenge, gay cartoons of red or green—always there must be something to destroy the white monotony. And yet you must not deface the cast yourself. That is for your visitors, your fellow patients, and the nurses in the ward. You must draw them into the conspiracy. Sometimes even the doctors can be incited to ruin their own alabaster art.

In my case it started with an itch. Inside the cast, on the outside of the knee—not the sliced and stitched ankle, where you might expect it, but the entirely unprovoked knee—my eczema flared. Just a little irritation, but that was all it took inside the sealed tomb of the cast: the skin's siren call—unreachable goal, insatiable desire. I itched the worst itch I would ever itch.

It was Uncle Dick who provided the means for my salvation. My mother's youngest brother, the only one of seven siblings to graduate from college (thanks to the GI Bill), he worked for Lockheed, maker of airplanes. When I went to the hospital, he gave me a book called *The Boy Engineer* and a white plastic slide rule. Perhaps Uncle Dick meant to inspire me with mathematics and science— Japanese are said to be good at that sort of thing—and indeed I soon made use of the slide rule or at least of the long, slim, flat blade that slid back and forth in a frame decorated with hash marks and numerals. I removed the shaft and poked it along my right thigh, down inside the cast, the blade's hard, sharp corner finding the hungry flesh along the knee and scraping, first gently, tentatively, then in long strokes of impassioned conviction. Oh, happy logarithm! Oh, sweet computation! And when at last I withdrew the blade, its tip damp with the clinging grit of broken skin and a smear of blood, I blessed my uncle and his gift.

But, oh, infection, fated consequence of bliss! The itch returned; and no matter how often and assiduously I applied the slide rule, my insistent flesh tantalized and tormented me. Finally, the surgeon had to cut again: this time not bone but plaster. His weapon looked like a circular saw, yet he told me the blade did not rotate but merely vibrated back and forth at devastating speed. He assured me that what felt like cutting of my skin was actually *burning*—heat from the friction of the blade vibrating against the resisting plaster. Was I supposed to find that information comforting? It did not help that the saw emitted a steady, high-pitched

eeeeeeeeeeeeeeeeeeeeeeeeeeeeeeeeeeeeeeeeeeeeeeeeeeeeeeeee,

the sinister song of a titanic mosquito. As powder from the cast whirled through the air, and dark lines sliced ever deeper through the white carapace, the saw scorching but not technically piercing my immobilized flesh, I clenched my teeth. (My dentist says I grind them even while I sleep.) The surgeon removed a three-inch square from the cast in the vicinity of the knee. Through that hole he washed and bandaged my abused skin, then cemented the white square back into place. The once-immaculate cast now had a darkly outlined, four-sided scar.

I never used the slide rule again.

Dick O'Leary was my best friend at the Shrine. We came to the hospital on the same day and left on the same day two months later. Dick had broken his left thighbone by slipping on ice while being chased by a girl on Sadie Hawkins' Day (or so he claimed); and while doctors were repairing the fracture, they discovered a cyst inside the bone. So he came to the Shrine to have a second operation in which surgeons chipped bone off his hip and used the detritus to fill the hole in his femur, like a dentist filling a cavity, but with living bone instead of dead silver or gold. After his operation Dick was in a full-body cast, plastered white from chest to foot, his thighs forming two sides of a triangle, and a stiff white pole from knee to knee forming the third. Above his bed hung a steel jungle of posts, beams, chains, bars. Dick would use these to swing around the bed like a Tarzan with legs of stone.

He could not get to the bathroom, and the bedpan was a challenge. His body cast had a large aperture behind. When the need arose, Dick would reach up, grab a bar dangling at the end of two chains, and pull himself high. Clinging with one hand, he would use the other to slide the bedpan into place beneath himself. Then, holding himself in position with both hands, as if for a pull-up, he would holler, "Bombs awaaaaaay!" He would perform more acrobatics to cleanse himself, then call out, "Nurse! Ward One!"

One day, though, something went awry. Maybe Dick was careless, maybe in too much of a hurry, maybe he was bushwhacked by the law of averages. Whatever the reason, he missed. Soon all the boys in the ward were howling for a nurse. My friend received a new nickname: Dead-Eye Dick.

There was another patient with whom I played, but after half a century I don't remember his name. He was my chess partner, but now I can't even remember his face. Maybe I never really looked. I think of him as dark-skinned—he may have been Indian or maybe Italian—with straight, dark hair and dark eyes that somehow gleamed. There was something about his deportment, quiet and withdrawn, that made him seem to exist in shadows. So let's just call him the dark boy.

He was lucky, in a way. He was the only patient at the Shriners Hospital for Crippled Children whose wheelchair was motorized. One night, when no nurses were in sight, the other boys lined up behind him, each holding onto the handles of the chair in front of his own. The dark boy's vehicle became a locomotive hauling a chain of cars. As the train rolled down the long, dimly lit hallway, clattering over the tile floor, it gradually picked up speed. Then the engineer wheeled suddenly around a corner, as sharply as possible, cracking the whip on the procession of wheelchairs behind. Then, woe to him in the caboose! Spinning to the side, tilting on one wheel, slamming against a wall, toppling out of your chair, and whirling in your pajamas across the icy floor—it's tough being a cripple.

Then everyone fled back to the wards, jumped into bed, and prepared a denial for the nurses. Sometimes after an incident like this, they would punish us by taking away our comic books. Sometimes a ringleader would get transferred to a different ward.

But not the dark boy. He would not be punished. Who could do that?

When I first came to the ward, the other boys told me he could not be beaten at chess. He was so good, no one would play against him. I knew only the rudiments of the game, but nevertheless I accepted his invitation to compete. I won two of our first three matches. I must have known more than I had thought, or maybe he wasn't as good as everybody said. After that, I played him every day.

He was fast. I mean, he didn't think long about each move. What took time was his hand, the right one, curled down at the wrist so that his stiff, straightened fingers formed a cone that descended over queen or castle to move it. As soon as I had finished my play, his thin forearm would reach across the board, and the hand like a mechanical claw would grasp the chesspiece, the same way it grasped the controls of his wheelchair. His other hand was useless, the left arm dangling withered at his side.

The dark boy must have gotten better. Day by day, he beat me more and more often, more and more easily, quicker and quicker, until finally I wouldn't play with him anymore. Then he went away.

For the dark boy, all of life was a game of chess. He knew the moves.

A few weeks after my operation, I had to surrender my wheelchair and graduate to crutches. The new toy was not as much fun as the other but also not without potential: you could raise the crutch to eye level and aim it at somebody like a rifle. "Pow! You're dead!"

After you got good with crutches, you could run. The trick was the hop. You would swing the crutches forward, use their tips as fulcrums to hurl your body ahead, then plant your one good foot on the ground. No, *plant* is the wrong word, for rooting yourself to earth was exactly the opposite of what you wanted to do. Rather, you would *bounce* your foot upon the ground, springing your body forward as far as possible before letting that same foot touch earth again. Only then, after the leap, would you resort to a second swing of the crutches. Using this method, a boy could attain a respectable velocity. I heard of one who ran a mile in seven minutes. I never came close to that, but I could run almost as fast on crutches as I could before my operation. The nurses, however, discouraged our footraces, especially indoors and shortly after surgery.

The second time the doctor cut my cast, it was for good: slicing straight down the front and back, then splitting the cast open like the shell of a peanut. My shocked leg was unprepared for liberation. After two months of disuse, the muscles had forgotten how to move. When the physical therapist forced my knee to bend, the pain from that manipulation colored all my senses white.

I was still on crutches when I went back to school, where I found that my catastrophe had made me a celebrity. Other students carried my books. Lovely Mary Ella called me on the phone and talked for an hour and a half. At softball games I was elevated to officialdom, bending forward behind the plate, crutches splayed diagonally from my armpits to the ground as I called balls and strikes.

One day at the end of class I forgot I couldn't walk. I slid from my seat behind one of those antique desks with its iron feet bolted to the floor—you remember them if you are as old as I and went to a school with a name like Washington Irving—desks with the names of children carved and penciled into the mottled wooden top and an empty inkwell making a round window into the desk's darkness. I stood up and took one step forward on my innocent leg; and after a long moment of startled awakening, like a pilot whose bomber has burst into flames, I crumpled to the floor. For another long moment everyone stared at me in surprise and confusion. Then someone helped me to my feet, and someone else retrieved my crutches from where they leaned in the corner of the classroom. I had never gotten so much attention in my life.

It must have been a great day when I could walk again; when, at last, without brace or cast or crutch, I took that historic first step with my right foot, followed quickly by the left, and then, after a pause for a small smile, the triumphant right again. It was one of the most important moments of my life and certainly the most suspenseful: probably a doctor or nurse or therapist, and probably my mother, watching hopefully, anxiously poised to reach out and catch me if I fell, but then, seeing me stride on and on, joining me in quiet rejoicing. I could walk! My life began anew! Yes, it must have been a wonderful moment, and I wish I could remember something about it.

All I actually know is that a few months after leaving the hospital, I could walk. It took more months before I could swing a bat or run the bases; but by the time eighth grade started, I could do even that—as well as I ever could, anyway. Now, however, it was without a brace.

My Right Foot

The operation that freed me from the brace exacted a price: an inch of flesh. I was only twelve, a growing boy, when I had the surgery. My left foot continued to grow; my right did not. Today my right foot is two shoe sizes smaller than my left, and my right leg an inch shorter. This is why I walk with a limp. This is also why, when I walk along the sloping shore, I like to have my left side facing the sea. With my longer leg treading the lower ground, my gait is almost normal.

When I walk on a flat surface, my right foot hits the ground off-plumb, tilted to the right. If you turned over my shoe and looked at its bottom, you would see that the rubber heel and leather sole are worn down more at the outer edge than the inner. Yet in comparison to the left shoe, the right seems hardly worn at all. As I walk, I quickly and unthinkingly shift my weight off the right foot and onto the left, so that after months of wear, the left sole may be thin as a playing card while the right is thick as a poker chip.

But shoes have no constitutional right to equal treatment. What does it matter if my gait is unbalanced and I lean to one side? What matters is that I can walk. What matters is that when I was thirty years old, I was playing left field in a softball game, and the batter hit a long fly toward the foul line to my right. I ran as fast as I have ever run, step after step after step, but without thinking about those steps or either of the feet taking them—without thinking about anything. I crossed my gloved left hand in front of me and reached out. What matters is that the ball smacked the webbing of my glove and stayed there. *Out!*

Is there a happiness greater than this? A sense of the universe being just exactly right? It doesn't matter that when my legs finally stopped churning, my right arm lofted a feeble throw to no one in particular, enabling a runner at third base to tag up and score. My teammates applauded my catch; and I, out of breath and with heart pounding, beamed.

It is good to have a foot that works.

Have I not told you that I walk upon the beach? I prefer the most distant and desolate shores, in winter when there's no one there but me. No mermaids sing to me, but I sing to them or shout poetry to the waves. "Roll on, thou deep and dark blue ocean—roll!" Sometimes I'll walk for miles in soft sand, sinking at every step into a tender trap from which I must extricate myself; and when I get home, my right ankle aches from the prolonged exertion. That's another reason I walk with a limp.

After my operation I stopped wearing orthopedic shoes and switched to ordinary ones in a variety of colors and styles: stiff black dress shoes, brown wing-tips, cordovan loafers, tennis shoes, moccasins, even sandals (held on by straps and buckles—*zori* are still impossible). I never wear high-tops, except for hiking boots. I used to have a friend in Nashville, another polio survivor, who swapped shoes with me. I wore a size eight left and size six right, he wore the opposite, and after buying two pairs of shoes—one pair in each size—we kept the shoes that fit us and mailed each other the mismatched leftovers. Without him I never would have had a pair of golf shoes or white bucks. Mostly, though, he sent me sneakers and walking shoes, and I wore them gratefully.

My operation worked for forty-one years. After the fusing of my ankle bones, I could walk without a brace. Sure, I walked with a limp, and the ankle hurt if I hiked too far or landed on the side of my foot when playing basketball in the driveway. But those were the minor, occasional aches of any middle-aged man. When I was fifty-three, however, I got a soreness in my ankle that would not desist. I went to a series of doctors: my primary-care physician, a podiatrist, a physiatrist (not psychiatrist, not yet, but a specialist in physical rehabilitation), an orthopedist specializing in legs, an orthopedist specializing in feet. (Are you old enough to have noticed that as you age, your doctors and dentists multiply?) The diagnosis was "advanced osteoarthritis"— an absence of cartilage in my ankle so that with every step, bone was scraping bone. My body was fulfilling its destiny, maturing into a ruin.

I tried hot baths and ace bandages, pills for pain and inflammation, dietary supplements and massage— everything but needles. My sister in California sent me little magnetic disks that attached to my ankle with adhesives, like medicated pads for removal of corns; and when I visited Japan, I wafted onto my ankle sanctified smoke at a Shinto temple, and I hoisted my foot to touch the hand of a wooden statue of a disciple of the Buddha.

Nothing worked. The foot surgeon told me he could perform an operation that might improve the ankle, but, then again, it might not; and it would incapacitate me for months. There was, however, another solution: easier, faster, cheaper, safer, painless, and sure.

A brace.

The long, hard sojourn of life is, I discovered, a circle. After four decades of freedom, I allowed my foot to be put back in chains. I hoped that the new brace would prove temporary, that it would provide my foot with a few weeks of rest that would heal it so I would never need a brace again. Months, however, brought no cure. At home I removed the brace, but even the mildest exertions— walking to the end of the driveway to retrieve the newspaper, going upstairs to bed or down to the basement with a load of laundry—brought pain that magnified my limp. After a year I realized that the brace was part of me again.

The new brace, however, is different from the old. Instead of steel, it is made of hard plastic—prosthetic post-modernism—and molded to wrap the back of my leg and bottom of my foot: from just below the knee, down the calf, around the heel, and out to the ball of my foot. My shin and the top of my foot are not covered by plastic. The brace is a translucent pale gray, and it is fastened to my leg by two wide strips of heavy, khaki-colored tape whose tips are secured not by steel buckles but by Velcro.

The new brace has a different purpose from the old: not to fix my foot in the shape of an L—the surgery did that—but to protect the ankle from constant jostling. The brace is a plastic shell within which nothing moves.

Another difference between the new brace and the old is that the new one is not permanently attached to one shoe. Instead it slips inside any shoe, or at least any one big enough to hold it. The device makes my foot seem a little wider and elevates it perhaps an eighth of an inch—a helpful boost for my short leg. To accommodate the brace, however, I had to throw out some of my shoes and buy new ones a half size larger. Because of this, I could no longer exchange shoes with my partner in Nashville.

Some of my new shoes have a special feature: an extra slab of rubber built into the sole and heel of the right shoe. This "lift," which adds half an inch to the thickness of the bottom of my shoe, attracts the attention of uniformed personnel at airport security, who bombard the shoe with X rays and dust it with powder to reveal traces of explosives. The lift also makes my right leg seem almost as long as my left and thereby reduces my limp. Moreover, the doctors say that making the legs nearly even will reduce stress on my spinal column and save me from backaches in later life. At my age, however, I wonder whether I shall live long enough for "later" to arrive.

My doctors want me to wear my specially tailored shoes almost all the time, but I do not comply. Instead I wear whatever footwear seems most appropriate for a particular occasion—not, as in my childhood, a single ubiquitous pair of shoes like a scarlet letter proclaiming disability. In good weather I usually put on sneakers: ordinary and off-the-shelf. Comfortably casual, they match my shorts or jeans. In snow or pouring rain I don heavy leather boots. Only when I dress up, wearing slacks, do I put on my orthopedically correct shoes. I seldom dress up.

I don't have a physiatrist anymore, not since my old one left for a post at Harvard. She literally wrote the book on post-polio syndrome, and before quitting private practice, she gave me lots of expert advice. She told me to go easy on my weakened body. She said I have a limited supply of strength and must be careful not to exhaust it. She said that walking was good for me, but I should stop every ten minutes to check my pulse and to rest. She had an occupational therapist teach me the least strenuous methods of getting out of bed and of getting off the floor in case I should fall down. The doctor suggested that I sit on a stool while taking a shower and that I install a taller toilet so I don't have to go so far to sit down or stand up. She said I could have the gas and brake pedals on my car relocated so I could operate them with my left foot, the stronger one. She offered to help me get a sticker for Handicapped Parking. She probably would not have liked it if she had seen me practicing lay-ups and jump shots at the basketball hoop in my driveway.

The doctor's advice represents the current orthodoxy for treatment of people who had polio, which is the opposite of what I learned in my youth. In those days I was urged to exercise strenuously to build strength in my damaged foot: use it or lose it. Now, however, the emphasis is on conservation of the body's energy, a resource in finite supply like coal or petroleum. The doctor is right, no doubt. Nevertheless, I choose to act as if my body were mechanically unimpaired. I refuse to forego my ordinary pleasures and labors in order to avert stress and the possibility of eventual exhaustion. I would rather limp than sit.

The essayist Montaigne seems to have anticipated the tidal reversals in treatment of polio survivors. The skeptical Frenchman said that medicine is an uncertain science and that while one physician may prescribe a particular remedy for an ailment, another physician will prescribe the opposite. Since there is no way of knowing which treatment will work best for you, Montaigne recommended that you choose the one requiring the least disruption of the life to which you have become accustomed, the life that you enjoy. Why undertake a therapy more loathsome than the illness it is meant to cure? It took more than four hundred years for me to get around to reading Montaigne; but by the time I finally did, I was already doing what he had suggested. Medical science has become much more reliable in the centuries since Montaigne lived. However, its authority is still not absolute, at least not for me.

See me, then, as I approach you on a typical day in June or September. I wear a baseball cap, perhaps featuring a red B for Boston or a teal and silver compass rose for the Seattle Mariners (I am a man of many caps). I wear clear glasses, not sunglasses, because I prefer to see true colors, especially on the birds or wildflowers I try to identify. I wear a T-shirt, perhaps the huge, garish Donald

Duck over broad horizontal stripes of red and black, that my wife brought me from Florida; or the dark green Kimo's Rules ("No Rain—No Rainbows") I bought in Hawaii. ("Kimo" is the Hawaiian equivalent of "Jim.") I wear shorts, maybe the blue ones with patch pockets in front and back and slash pockets on the side. I like to have many pockets for the souvenirs I find on my walks and the notes I write to myself.

Beneath my bare right knee you see two khaki bands across my white sock. Unless you are a professional in orthopedics, however, you probably will not notice that I bend my left leg slightly at the knee, even when putting all my weight upon it, instead of straightening it out as I do with my right. This makes the left leg seem almost as short as the right. I was not aware that I was bending my knee until the man who made my new brace pointed it out.

If you glance back after passing me and observe me from behind, you might see the tall plastic brace, translucent gray, broad at the top of the calf, narrowing as it goes down to the ankle, then disappearing into the back of my white sneaker. If you watch me take a few steps, you might notice that I limp. However, if you think about it, you might also notice that the limp does not prevent me from sauntering about the neighborhood.

But did you hear me? Did you hear the squeak? My brace does not fit perfectly tightly into some shoes and is not cemented into place. Therefore, the brace's heel slips slightly with every step, massaging the inside of the sneaker to produce a small, sibilant, soprano squeal.

Listen,   and   you'll   know   it's   me.

Chapter Two

❈ Confessions of a Bronze Adonis ❈

You can't help but notice my largest organ. From April to October I display it to the neighbors as I shoot baskets in the driveway. My purpose, however, is not to expose it to people but to the sun.

I refer, of course, to my skin. I wear short pants and no shirt when exercising in the heat. I would not say that I am comfortable in my skin, but I do say that I have found ways to enjoy it.

My wife calls me her "Bronze Adonis." She jests, obviously, since my physique will not remind you of the youth over whom amorous and jealous goddesses contended. But when Barbara calls me "Your Bronzeness," she speaks the truth, at least in summer. As much as the weather and the law allow, I toast my skin before the distant bonfire of the sun, replacing the pallor of winter with . . . well, what? I look at the back of my hand and find ruddy, brown, and olive tones, but then I turn my palm up and see splotches of pink. So no one word will do justice to my epidermis in August, though I suppose that *bronze* is as true as any. Perhaps it is more of an ideal than an achievement.

But I am no mere sybarite forever idling under the sweetly smiling sun as if the great outdoors were a gigantic tanning salon. No, not at all. I combine pleasure with labor, though, in truth, it's hard to distinguish between the two. Mostly I read. On warm days I sit on a cushioned metal chair, my bare feet resting on the bench that serves as a railing around the deck at the rear of our house, away from the curious street. I wear an old baseball cap to shade my eyes, as well as profoundly tinted reading glasses. I wear shorts or swim trunks but no shirt, and I hold a book in my lap. Atop a hollow metal pole that spears the bull's-eye of a circular metal-mesh table on which I set my ballpoint pen, there is a large white parasol; but I almost never open it. I prefer the sun.

I was born in Spokane, a city named after an Indian tribe whose name means Children of the Sun. Now I live on the opposite side of the continent, in the land of the Wampanoags, People of the First Light. Do you discern a pattern here? I was born for old Sol.

I am a heliotrope. On my deck on a summer morning I face east as the sun rises over the trees. At mid-day I move to a chair facing south. Partly this is to shield the page I'm reading from the glare of the sun, but partly it's to expose my face and chest to that same glare. The warmth goes through to my soul or at least my lungs. In the late afternoon, when the house shades the deck from the westering sun, I step down to the back yard and sit upright on a chaise longue, pivoting it like a compass needle so that I always face the sun.

Of course there are parts of me that never see the day. Well, almost never. A few years ago some friends invited me to join them at a "clothing-optional" beach on Cape Cod. I opted to keep my swim trunks on, but then I noticed that everyone else was naked. Shy as I am, I did not want to call attention to myself; so I, too, impersonated Adam. One of the younger, more buxom women wore nothing but a hat she had bought at a flea market, and everybody stood in a circle around her, saying how nice it looked. I tried to keep my eyes on people's faces for the entire afternoon. I do not say that I succeeded.

Sunlight is said to trigger the conjugal instinct in birds, with the ever-longer days of spring stimulating development of avian gonads, provoking the creatures to perform mating dances or migrate to distant breeding grounds. All this may be true, but I am not a bird. I have other reasons to love the sun.

Barbara worries about skin cancer and wants me to apply sun-block as she does. She is right, no doubt; but I point out that sometimes when my eczema is at its bloody worst, my dermatologist prescribes ultraviolet radiation— the rays repair the shattered skin—and what is sunbathing but natural radiology? Then, too, sunlight is a source of Vitamin D, and I soak it up like a painted turtle basking on a log in a pond. Besides, I believe that people with naturally dark complexions like mine are less vulnerable to the sun than are the fairer children of Eve, so why not

A Piece of Valiant Dust

make the most of it? Why give up our only advantage? The odds of getting melanoma are long, after all. My skin already gives me enough to worry about.

My skin records my life, largely in the form of scar tissue. What is a scar but an aide-mémoire, a reminder of the past afflictions our flesh has survived and of the future ones it will not?

My record begins with a birthmark, a dark red splotch on the inside of my left thigh. Actually it is an archipelago of splotches, with two principal islands and half a dozen lesser ones, some little more than reefs lying offshore. The largest island, shaped like the voluptuous leaf at the center of the ace of spades (but more red than black), is three inches from its sharp apex to the base of its thick stem. The other large island, two inches at its widest point, consists of two circles with a bridge between them, looking like a pair of sunglasses or a sagging brassiere, depending on your fancy. You might expect the birthmark to grow less noticeable as the skin around it tans in summer, but the opposite is true: it grows darker, purple, luminous, and more conspicuous. My stigmata give small children something to think about when they see me in shorts. Still, I am grateful not to have the birthmark on my face.

My favorite scar is on my stomach, roughly equidistant between navel and left nipple. You can scarcely see it anymore, a brown welt the size of a large split pea. I got it when I was five or six, sliding down a banister, rear end first, from our upstairs apartment to the front door. A splinter of wood tore loose from the banister and stabbed into and under the skin of my gut. A doctor—laughing, my mother recalls—removed the sliver and stitched the hole, but what I remember most vividly was the shot he gave me first. How can you forget a needle being thrust into your belly? Later I heard that people being treated for possible rabies infection had to receive multiple injections in their stomachs; and, judging from my own experience, I always imagined that therapy to be almost as horrible as rabies itself.

I have had my share of infections. Once, when I was eight or ten, staphylococcus invaded my skin. Blisters erupted on my arms and legs, especially in the soft tissue inside the elbows and knees. I was taken to the hospital and placed in an isolation ward. I remember taking baths in water turned black by an antibiotic. Nurses, wearing rubber gloves, would gently squeeze the pustules, adding their cloudy fluid to the dark water. After a week I got out of the hospital, and my skin slowly healed, the new pink patches (where the boils had been) turning in time to the normal light brown.

Years later my mother told me it had been a close call. If the infection had spread into my blood stream, the doctors had told her, I would have died. The boy in the room next to mine did.

At the time, I didn't realize that anyone was dying or that I might, too. That's how it often is: death is right next door, and you don't even know it. I suppose that if I brooded about this—about how Time's winged chariot is swooping down upon me—I might dedicate myself to living with a special intensity. Montaigne says that because he knows his span on earth will be short, he tries to exploit it fully, the proximity and certainty of death adding a piquancy to the pleasure of living. I, however, am less philosophical, less deliberate, less given to rational planning, than he. I would prefer not to think about my impending demise. If I attempt to extract as much flavor from life as I can, it is not because I am in a desperate race against death. It is merely because I enjoy living. I take my hedonism direct, not magnified by reflection.

Lucretius, a follower of Epicurus, wrote a book called *The Nature of Things*. He said that gods pay no attention to us human beings, so we should pay them back in kind. We should attend instead to other things—*Things*—and make the most of them. I believed all that when I was a youth, long before I had heard of Lucretius or Epicurus.

"Don't it always seem to go," Joni Mitchell used to sing to me, "that you don't know what you got till it's gone?" But she exaggerated. In order for you to appreciate something, it doesn't have to slam the screen door, slouch into a Big Yellow Taxi, and ride away forever. It just has to malfunction. That's when you realize how much you use it and how badly you need it.

The staph infection that sent me to the hospital was one I probably got by scratching, and I owed that scratching to eczema. Egg-ZEE-muh is what I called it when I was little. Now I have learned to say ECK-zih-muh. That's what college does for you. But no matter what I call it, it's always the same. Eczema taught me the meaning of the word *chronic*. It also taught me to observe what, otherwise, would have gone unnoticed all around me. Namely, my skin.

When I was a child and my mother put me to bed, she would slip heavy socks over my hands and fasten them at the wrists with rubber bands. If she did not do that, I would scratch sheets of skin from my arms and legs, even while asleep. During my waking hours I had no such protection, other than a willpower I exercised only sporadically. Many is the time my shirtsleeves have been spotted with blood.

My brother and I shared a bedroom, and sometimes he would startle me with a sudden, loud command during the night: "Quit scratching!" My scratching was so vigorous that the sound of it would keep him awake, though his bed was on the other side of the room from mine. Fingernails grating across dry skin can produce a noise that fills an otherwise silent chamber; and when the noise ceases only for a minute or two, then resumes again and yet again, it can drive one to fury. "*Quit* scratching!" my brother would stubbornly shout. "I can't help it," I would futilely explain.

The eczema is not as severe today as in my childhood, but it never goes away. There is always some part of my body—the lower back, the jaws, the calf, the belly where the beltbuckle scrapes against it—that is inflamed. Sometimes I get little boils on my scalp in the back of my head, and scratching swells them into rolling hills of subtly throbbing pain. In hot, humid weather my sweaty throat sprouts rubbery red bumps the size of aspirin tablets; and I can't resist clawing my fingernails across them, creating garish crimson streaks.

The eczema has made me appreciate my hands. Mostly from July to December, in spells that last for months at a time, the skin on the fingers and in the palms grows dry as old leather, cracks open or peels off, leaving tiny red arroyos and basins ready to fill with pain. When I slice an onion, the juice from it stings. When I squeeze a wedge of lime for a gin-and-tonic, I atone through suffering for my indulgence. Sometimes my fingertips grow so swollen and sore that it hurts me to button a shirt. I had never realized how hard a button is, compared to the poor, frail flesh that must press against it.

Once, I had a dream about my face. A fleck of skin the size of a baby's fingernail was peeling from the cheek, beneath the eye. I pinched the flake, brittle and brown as the epidermis of an onion, between my thumb and forefinger, and plucked it away. But it left behind rough edges, imperfections, like a bad paint job. So I carefully tore away the entire layer of integument to make my face flawless again and whole.

Whole? A bad pun, because it was then that I discovered, beneath that first curling flake, a tiny puncture, black, like a spot of mold. So I tore away that sheet, too; the skin—thicker now than before—coming off in broad strips like the flesh of an onion. But the hole was still there, and larger. I removed another layer, but the hole only got wider, a broadening circle of black; and other tunnels opened, on my forehead, alongside my ear, between my eyes. As I peeled away the cold tissue, the voids grew larger, enormous, till my face was a fragile ruin and at last I realized that underneath that devastated surface there was nothing at all.

I have heard that every human body produces a bounteous daily crop of dead skin that peels off and feeds an army of tiny mites inhabiting our bedsheets and mattresses. I suspect, however, that my body produces more than most. This is especially true of my scalp, which yields dandruff that I harvest with an efficiency bordering on the industrial.

I sit with my head leaning over a smooth, dark surface—an oak coffee table or, better still, a black-cherry desk—dark so it may serve as a foil for the pale treasure I am about to manufacture. Using both hands, I scrape my fingernails across my scalp, loosening and dropping white flakes beyond number. Then, as if switching from coarse sandpaper to fine, I scratch vigorously with the soft tips of my fingers, rubbing free an even tinier detritus. This makes my scalp tingle. Next, with fingers straight and palms down, I slap back and forth across my head, the two hands slicing through my hair in opposite directions. This shakes loose those bits of skin that had been clinging to the hair, as if I were threshing grain.

By this time the tabletop is powdered with pale motes of various shapes and sizes. Three or four times I drag my stiff right forefinger across the sprinkled surface, right to left, organizing the lumpy dust into a long, straight ridge. (I'm told that people do something like this with cocaine.)

Then I sweep my finger down the ridge from top to bottom, as if to collapse the line of powder into a single point. I prod the sides with my fingertip, rounding off the edges, until I have created a tidy mound, a miniature Fujiyama of dead skin. I study it for a moment. "That," I say to myself, "is me." Then, as if blowing out a candle, I puff it off the table, scattering it onto the carpet, where it becomes invisible. Eventually it will find a home in the vacuum. Dust to dust.

Of course I have gotten therapy for my skin. On my scalp I use a medicated shampoo. For the rest of my body I have had tests in which doctors turned my back into a grid and injected into each little square a dab of food or fabric, oil or pollen, to try to provoke an allergic reaction. The tests revealed many hazards for me to avoid: milk, wheat, pepper, grapefruit, wool, pine cones, cats, and, in short, creation. I have gotten allergy shots which at first had no effect but which after several weeks caused my arms to swell so painfully I had to stop the treatment. I have taken many kinds of pills, generation after generation of wonder drugs, but none that could prevent or abort the itching. In the end, all I can do is to rub cortisone ointment onto the broken skin to ameliorate the symptoms of the disease. There is no cure.

That's life, or at least *my* life, but it's not as miserable as you might think. If you don't have eczema, you probably aren't aware of its delights. Without an itch, you never get the satisfaction of a scratch, a satisfaction often seized but rarely, if ever, acknowledged. Where is our gratitude? Glory be to God for eczema!

It's hard to say what causes the original itch: a chemical reaction to something in the air, perhaps; the chili you ate for lunch or the lemon you squeezed over the fillet of sole at dinner; maybe the dry air that dehydrates your skin; or maybe the humidity that makes you sweat; or perhaps it is only the sheer, blind operation of chance. Whatever the cause, you feel a slight irritation on the surface of your body, so, without a thought, without interrupting for more than a second whatever you were doing—reaching across the table for the salt, say, or combing your hair in front of the bathroom mirror—you soothe the irritation by rubbing your fingertips across it, your fingers curled but rigid, so that the edges of your nails rake your skin. Sometimes that is enough, the itch goes away, and you resume whatever you were doing.

But sometimes that is only the beginning. The itch persists, your brief scratch only having aggravated it, further irritating the skin and provoking you to scratch again, harder. Now you have begun the process of excavation, peeling off the dry outer layer of skin and getting down to what is pink and moist and alive. And still you persevere, noting the dark grit forming tiny balls on the surface of your skin or accumulating beneath your fingernails. As the itch becomes more intense, so does the pleasure you feel as your fingers dig. You observe that you have begun to bleed, and you know you ought to stop scratching because that only makes the itch worse; but you do not stop. Indeed, you only stop whatever you were doing before, eating dinner or dressing for work, because now you must devote yourself entirely to scratching.

The tips of your fingers are damp. You know that for the next few days your face or throat or wrist will display unsightly red streaks, maybe followed by scabs, and that your collar or sleeves may be stained by blood. But still you scrape. And why? Why do you do what you know will harm you, what all your years of experience show will only make matters worse? Why do you continue to gouge your own dear flesh?

Because nothing in the world feels better than this!

Yes, I shall tell you what many people know but none admits: scratching, hard scratching, scratching to draw blood, to break the flesh, to turn your body into meat— this kind of scratching is a joy. The feeling that radiates from that parcel of violated skin is sweet. The itch is salty, but the scratch is sweet. As your fingers do their nasty work, you may close your eyes; and though your teeth may be clenched, the corners of your mouth just might turn up in a tight, ecstatic smile. And the word to which I keep returning to describe what you're feeling is *sweet*. Something gentle but insistent pulses happiness all through you. Sweet, sweet, sweet.

That is, of course, a religious word. The mystics say that in the presence of God they are swept up in a torrent of sweetness. I claim neither divine nor diabolical origins for eczema, but I do believe that it can teach us about sin. Think of scratching as a sin, not the original one but probably not far behind. You know you should not do it, you do not want to, and yet you cannot resist. At the time

44

you do it, the time of bliss, you feel as close to paradise as you'll ever get. And so you do it and do it and do it. You can repent later when the dermatologist gives you a new prescription.

Scratching is not the only pleasure to be derived from eczema. Let us say that the inside of your wrist, with the large veins running through, has been irritated by your watchband chafing it. You scratch until the skin is raw, and still the itch does not subside. So what do you do?

You walk to the bathroom sink, twist the knob on the left, then place your abused wrist under the stream of water. The fluid is instantly soothing, but after it gets extremely hot, it produces a thrill that shoots up your spine to the top of your skull. You run the water until it is scalding, you can scarcely bear it, your wrist is turning red, but you keep it under the faucet just the same.

Finally, however, you are exhausted, the pain is too much. You withdraw your hand, turn off the one faucet, and turn on the other. When the stream has grown truly cold, like ice water, you thrust your wrist into it and feel a chill that makes you close your eyes. The itch is gone, at least for now.

Pruritus is another word for itch. Eczema might be the original prurience.

There was once a philosopher named Chin Sheng-t'an who wanted at all times to keep one or another part of his body inflamed with eczema, just so he could pour hot water over it. "Ah," he exclaimed, "is this not happiness?" I would have thought that such a Kama Sutra of dermatitis would have been written by a Japanese. Aren't they—

we—supposed to be the world's premier connoisseurs of the sensual, the boldest explorers in the pleasures of the flesh? Perhaps the Chinese were the pioneers after all, and the Japanese mere copycats.

But how does it end, this itching? You can't always calm an inflammation with hot and cold running water, and even that form of soothing eventually wears off. Scratching only makes the itch worse, so how does it end, and why?

No one knows. It just does. You have scratched for pleasure, scratched yourself bloody, and gotten as much gratification from that as you can. Now the scratching is just a bother. So you try to ignore the itch, keep your hands off yourself, read a book or, better still, mow the lawn. You lapse once in a while, scrape the sore, but then catch yourself and exert self-restraint again. Then, miraculously, for no apparent reason, the itch disappears. You don't notice when it goes away, any more than you notice the moment at which you fall asleep. It just happens.

Life resumes.

Chapter Three

❊ American Dilemmas ❊

When I was growing up in Spokane, Washington, I learned there were three kinds of people: *nihonjin*, *hakujin*, and *kurombos*. Nihonjin means "Japanese people," ones from Nihon, also called Nippon. Hakujin means "white people." In Japan they're called *gaijin*, "foreign people," but it would be presumptuous to call them that in America. Kurombos means "blacks"—the suffix implying "people" is meaningfully omitted. The Japanese are not the most egalitarian of peoples.

Japanese, whites, blacks—these, then, were the three races of Spokane. I guess there would be four if you included my Boy Scout buddy Joe McCormack, a direct descendant of Chief Joseph of the Nez Perces, but there weren't enough Indians in the city for the Japanese to need a name for them. Joe was the only Indian I knew, and I lost track of him when he joined the marines. Of course, I saw the Spokane Indians as often as I could, but they were just a baseball team, a farm club of the Dodgers. Most of the real Spokane Indians were on a reservation far from town. My mother used to think they were kept there like prisoners in a concentration camp, but I told her they could leave if they wanted to. I wonder how she got that idea?

In Spokane it was hard to find even the *history* of the native people. Half a mile west of my house, for example, ran a stream that everybody called Hangman Creek, even though its name on the map was Latah. I never knew why it was called Hangman until, decades after leaving home, I read about it in a history book. Along the creek's banks in 1858 the army had strung up six Palouses and a Yakima on charges of rebellion, meaning that they had resisted when whites took over their country. Near the creek was a place called Indian Canyon. A diminishing number of Spokanes had lived there as late as the 1920s, but by the time I was born, they were gone. In my day the canyon was home to a golf course, not Indians.

There also were no white ethnics in Spokane, at least none of whom I was aware. It wasn't until I went east for college that I learned to note the precise country from which a white person's ancestors had come. I suppose I had heard that Karen Sackville-West was of English stock; Art Murphy, Irish; Christina Van Veen, Dutch; but it never occurred to me that anyone might *care* about these national origins. Danny Malet pronounced his last name like a hammer, so how was I to know he was French?

Was Joanne Gould Jewish? I heard years later that Gail Gotzian was, but her religion didn't seem to damage her popularity. She was voted Football Princess, and I thought she was gorgeous. Joel Lassman, my classmate in grade school, was definitely Jewish; and everybody knew it because he got extra holidays from school. It didn't seem fair. Nobody teased him, but perhaps that was just because he was the strongest boy in the neighborhood. The last time I saw him—it was on TV—he was playing fullback for Navy. The point is that as far as I was concerned, he was white. Japanese did not perceive ethnic distinctions among whites any more than we would among blacks. Maybe people who lived up on Rockwood Boulevard cared about religion or even ancestral nationality; but where I lived, at the bottom of Oak Street, it didn't matter.

Race was different. Race mattered. Race determined what you did every day: where you went and sometimes even how you felt. Our nameless neighborhood was mostly white, but with an enclave of Japanese. Our church, however, was in a more heterogeneous part of the city, where whites, blacks, and Japanese lived on the same block, though rarely in the same house. When we walked to church on a warm, sunny day, we would sometimes see an old black woman named Matilda sitting on her porch. We waved to her and she to us, but we never saw the inside of her house.

Blacks and Japanese didn't have much to do with one another. My high school had black students, and I did wrestle once in PE class with one who played halfback on the football team. He was merciful, handling me like a baby, so I escaped injury and even pain, though not a swift defeat. Aside from that, however, I saw black people only in class or in the halls. I heard of one Japanese woman who married a black man, but they lived on the other side of town. I don't remember ever meeting them. My mother says that people of her generation, the *nisei*, born in the United States, liked the black man and were friendly with the couple, but many in the immigrant generation, the *issei*, shunned them.

Not all the nisei, however, looked benignly upon the mixing of Japanese with a presumably inferior race. When I went away to college, my Auntie Toko—her real name was Tomiko, but her niece and nephews shortened it for her—Toko warned me not to come back with a white girl. She needn't have worried. By the time she died nineteen years later, with me still single, she probably would have welcomed any girl at all. Things had changed.

Janice, my sister, dated a few white guys in high school but never seriously. In college, though, she started going with an Anglo-Saxon named James Andrew Price; and after graduating, she married him. My mother said, "With initials like that, he can't be all bad." Jim said a nun had been the first person to point out to him his initials' sinister significance. Jan and Jim got married in our church and had the reception there, too, a reception with cake and coffee and not one drop of alcohol.

Our church was Methodist, and it was one of two Japanese churches in Spokane. The other was Buddhist, but there was not much difference between the two. Once a year the Buddhist kids would go to the Methodist church, and the Methodist kids would go to the Buddhist. We learned that the churches had different rituals but the same beliefs. Be nice to everybody, and don't forget to pray—that was the theology. In many families some children attended the Methodist church and others the Buddhist. You went wherever your best friends went. Once my hakujin friend Tom came to church with me, and afterward he said it was not at all what he had expected from a Methodist church. No ranting. Feeble singing. Kind of a bore, I guess. The two churches were not essentially Methodist or Buddhist. They were essentially Japanese. Our church had one white parishioner, which I think was one more than the Buddhist church had. Neither had kurombos. It was all about race.

"But the Japanese are not a race!" you object. "They're just a nationality, an ethnic group." To you I quietly and patiently reply: You did not live in Spokane in the 1950s. There the Japanese were a race, as much as the blacks or the whites. There must have been Chinese in Spokane, but I don't remember meeting any. Not to mention Koreans. The Vietnamese and Cambodians wouldn't come till a generation later, so the Japanese had sole occupancy of an entire racial category. You would not talk about "Asians" or even "Orientals." You would say, "Japanese." That's assuming you were polite. Jap! Nip! Yellow Monkey! These were the names thrown at me and my friends, along with rocks, when white boys from outside the neighborhood invaded. It was an unfair fight because although we had our own arsenal of stones, we were not armed with racial epithets to hurl back. How do you accuse your enemies of being white? They would take it as a compliment. Life is not fair.

Spokane had hundreds of Japanese because of the war. Before Pearl Harbor, the Japanese lived mostly near the

Pacific coast—my mother and father grew up in Portland, Oregon. Only a few nihonjin lived in Spokane. But then the government made the Japanese move to concentration camps (politely known at the time as "relocation centers"), then a couple years later released most of them to cities of the interior like Spokane, three hundred miles from the sea, almost in Idaho. My mother and her sister Fumi got out of camp by securing jobs as the upstairs and downstairs maids for a family on Spokane's South Hill. There the United States no longer had to worry that Nami and Fumi would dynamite ammo dumps or send secret radio messages to Jap submarines lurking offshore. Thus the Yellow Peril arrived in the Heart of the Inland Empire.

"Camp," I called it, because that's the word Mom always used. It struck me as strange. For me "camp" meant where I went with the Boy Scouts each summer: a week-long ordeal of tipping over canoes and filling the air with buckshot as clay pigeons arced unscathed across the sky. But when Mom said, "camp," the word meant something else.

The war cost Mom's family their chance to be Fred Meyer. That's the name of a chain of supermarket/department stores in the Pacific Northwest. In the 1930s Mom and her brothers and sisters sold produce in a street market in Portland. One of my mother's chores, of whose onerousness she later informed her slothful children, was shelling peas. How many hours does it take to fill a steel bucket with peas? What she hated even more was washing and trimming green onions, crates of them, on a Friday, so that on Saturday she would still smell of onions when she went to a dance.

Eventually the family had enough regular customers to buy a small store, a "mom & pop," except that their mom had died of tuberculosis and their pop of a stroke, so Uncle Bob, the first-born child, was the legal proprietor. Just a few years earlier in the same city, Fred Meyer had opened his first grocery.

Uncle Bob headed a family of seven siblings. Many people in Portland's Japanese community thought that was too much responsibility for a twenty-year-old, and they urged him to send the three youngest children—Hank, Nami, and Dick—to Japan to be raised by relatives. Uncle Bob, however, insisted on keeping his brothers and sisters together. Had he not done so, my mother would have been in Japan when the war broke out, and she would not have been able to return to America.

Uncle Bob was smart. Once when I was back in Spokane for a visit and had had a few drinks, I recited poetry to the gathered family after dinner. As I finished some verses from Chaucer, Bob announced, "That's *The Canterbury Tales*. The General Prologue." I was amazed. Bob had finished high school fifty years earlier and had not read poetry since, but he remembered his Chaucer.

Bob also had flair. Once we went to a Spokane Indians baseball game, and he got chosen for a contest between innings. He knew how to throw a baseball because he had played outfield on his high school team. Now, standing between the pitcher's mound and home plate, he was supposed to try to toss the ball through a round hole in a large, rectangular wooden target at second base. However, he decided to warm up by playing catch with the first baseman, making exaggerated gestures with each toss, like a clown. Finally, after prompting by impatient officials, he turned toward second base, tilted back till he almost fell over, teetered for a moment, then propelled his body forward and lobbed the ball. He missed the target, but the crowd cheered for him, hollering "Bob! Bob!" He raised his arms in triumph as he was escorted off the field.

Uncle Bob was hard-working and outgoing. His grocery might have been a great success, leading to who knows what expansions, acquisitions, diversifications, consolidations. Then again, it might have flopped—most small businesses do—or Bob might have spent forty years toiling as the proprietor of a corner grocery in Portland. We'll never know what would have happened, because the Japanese bombed Pearl Harbor.

Business fell off right away. Mom tells of an Indian, a longshoreman, who used to shop at their grocery every week with his wife. One day shortly after the war began, the woman came into the store while her husband waited outside. She said that his union had forbidden its members to shop at businesses owned by Japanese. The woman, crying as she explained this, bought enough groceries to fill their car. Then the couple drove away and never came back. Uncle Bob could see the handwriting on the wall, so he sold the store, down to the fixtures and the delivery truck.

Then came the evacuation. The government ordered all the nihonjin living near the Pacific coast—more than a hundred thousand of them, two-thirds of them born in the United States—to leave. On one of the last days Mom would spend in high school, her English teacher, Mrs. Winifred C. Hays, author of a writing textbook called *From Trail to Highway*, spent the entire class period talking about the relocation. She said that it was unconstitutional, that the Japanese—her students—were citizens who were being denied their rights, deprived of their property and freedom, without having committed a crime, without having even been *charged* with a crime. Mom was glad Mrs. Hays spent the whole hour talking about the evacuation, because the teacher never got around to making a homework assignment. Only later did Mom think about the content of the lecture. "It's unconstitutional," Mrs. Hays kept saying. "It's against the Constitution."

Nonetheless, it happened.

After the war Uncle Bob got a job as a baggage handler for the railroad. That was one of the few jobs open to Japanese men. Later he got a second job driving a delivery truck for a dry cleaner, but he never went into business for himself again.

Fred Meyer did better.

My mother's first stop in exile was the Portland Assembly Center, formerly known as the stockyards. Each family had its own stall, with walls that did not reach the ceiling, so you could hear what all the families around you were doing. The cattle were gone, but their odor was not so easy to remove. Dysentery swept through the center. My mother, however, caught such a bad case of the *flu* that her sister Tomi cried because she thought Mom was going to die.

When Uncle Bob heard that a brand-spanking-new concentration camp was being built at Tule Lake, at the northern tip of California, he volunteered to relocate the family there immediately. Most of the other Japanese from Portland chose to stay in their hometown as long as possible, hoping to remain there together. Eventually, though, the government dispersed them to various camps, which is how my father and his family ended up at Minidoka, in Idaho. My mother's family, however, had left Portland earlier, as pioneers of the diaspora, herded onto a train with windows shuttered (so that a hostile populace could not see who was inside) and transported south to Tule Lake.

Tule Lake was the largest of the relocation centers, holding almost nineteen thousand evacuees by the end of 1944. There also were five hundred civilians working there (not counting the Japanese) and twelve hundred soldiers standing guard. The camp had barbed-wire fences, twenty-eight watch towers, and eight tanks patroling the perimeter to keep the inhabitants under control. Tule Lake wasn't technically a prison, but it almost looked like one.

I drove there many years later with my Uncle Hank, who was revisiting scenes of his youth. There was nothing romantic there, though, nothing to be nostalgic about: just a desert with mountains in the distance. I didn't see any lake, though I suppose it was only a few miles away. The lake is a gathering place for waterfowl migrating from Wrangel Island (north of Siberia) down to Mexico. On a given day in the fall, you might see a million ducks and geese floating in rafts half a mile long. That's assuming you were at the actual lake instead of in the camp named after it. Concentration camps aren't ordinarily built on lakefront property. Hank said that summers in camp were dry and windy, and sand would blow into the barracks by passing beneath the poorly fitted doors. We inspected a few wooden buildings that had been preserved as a memorial, with a stone monument in front.

Camp.

Camp may have ruined my mother's trust in guns. I don't know for sure about this, but I got an inkling when I was a child. One day when my brother and sister had gone to school and I was alone at home with Mom, we played Guns. That's what we called it in my neighborhood: not "Cowboys and Indians" or "Cops and Robbers" but just plain "Guns." There was no need to fabricate a set of roles, a conflict of interests, a rationale for violence; we knew that the point was simply to shoot people. So I aimed my pistol at my mother's face and shouted, "Bang!" She told me not to point the gun at her. I asked how I could shoot her if I didn't aim at her. She said she didn't know, but don't do it, just pretend. It wasn't much fun playing Guns with Mom. I had to wait until my brother, Bob (named after my uncle), came home.

Often Bob and I played with Bryan and Larry, Japanese brothers who lived a block from us. Sometimes we played teams, sometimes every man for himself. The object of the game, of course, was to kill the other guy, but the hard part was to persuade the other guy that he had been killed. You could do it if you snuck up on him and opened fire from behind or from the side: "Bam-bam-bam! You're dead." But if you faced each other at the same time and both opened fire, each would claim that he had hit the enemy and that the enemy had missed himself. "You missed me, you missed me!" "No, I didn't. I got you!" In the game of Guns, shootings led to arguments, instead of vice versa. I guess you don't have that problem if you're using real guns.

I always liked guns—the toys, I mean. I used them so hard they broke in a few weeks, but over the span of my childhood I had dozens of them. I had a "Fanner Fifty," a revolver with a wide flange flaring back from the hammer like a thumb. You held the gun in one hand and slapped ("fanned") the flange back with the palm of the other hand in order to shoot quickly again and again. If you had a roll of caps, you could fill the air with noise and smoke. I had a trademark Sergeant Bilko pistol—a nice, heavy, silver automatic; but I didn't like it much because Sergeant Bilko was a funnyman on television who never shot anybody, so how could you take his gun seriously? I much preferred the signature weapon of The Rifleman. On his show he shot people all the time. Like the Fanner Fifty, The Rifleman's weapon was capable of rapid fire, automatically going off as soon as you finished cocking it, almost as good as a machine gun.

I also had a green plastic hand-grenade, but it was disappointing. When it hit the ground, all it set off was a single powder-filled cap. The tiny, tidy "Pop!" did not do justice to a weapon whose vast explosion hurled death in all directions. Water balloons were better.

When I got older, I had a real gun—a .22-caliber pellet gun anyway, a pistol. I would insert a slug into a chamber at the back, pump a rod beneath the barrel as if operating a bellows, to compress the air that would propel the pellet, then fire away at cans in the basement. Sometimes a friend and I would go out and shoot birds. My buddy told me that English sparrows and European starlings were exotics that were multiplying so rapidly they were driving the native birds to extinction, so it was all right to kill the intruders. (Today English sparrows are called "house sparrows," the invaders having triumphed so thoroughly as to become domesticated.) With his pellet rifle my friend would shoot a sparrow or starling out of a tree. Then, when the creature was on the ground and squirming, possibly dying but possibly only dazed, I would walk up to it, place the muzzle of my pistol to its head, and finish it off. The executioner.

But that was when I was in high school. Before that, when I was eight or ten, my brother and I had many water-guns—German *Lugers*, snub-nosed revolvers, and, my favorite, a black submachine gun that fired a stream over great distances. It didn't blast as much water as a garden hose, but it was more fun to use because it was a gun. Feeding into its stock was a rubber tube connected to a tank of extra ammunition that I carried on my back.

One day, though, Bob and I came home from school and discovered that all our squirt-guns were gone—not the cap-guns, fortunately, but all the squirt-guns. Mom had thrown them away. I don't remember what reason she gave, though I suppose it was our turning the house into a watery free-fire zone. Today she says she can't remember disposing of our arsenal.

I never found out what she had against guns. I'm not sure *she* knows. However, I invented my own explanation by remembering a story she had told us about camp.

It was a cloudless Sunday afternoon, and Mom and some friends went for a stroll. They walked out an open gate, away from camp, through an empty field, toward nothing in particular, just the world. Suddenly a young man appeared before them, a soldier in uniform. He yelled, "Halt!" then told them to go back. He spoke quietly and politely, but he carried a rifle. Mom discovered that she wasn't just "relocated." She was in jail. A gun made her feel the iron in the walls around her.

The evacuation occurred during Mom's senior year, making her miss the final weeks of class, but the high school mailed a diploma to her in camp anyway. The school also sent a copy of the yearbook, which had been passed around for her classmates to sign. In most yearbooks people say they are going to miss you, but in Mom's they say they have missed her for weeks. Nobody protests against the relocation, however, and hardly anyone even mentions it specifically. Instead they merely lament an inevitable, unnamed disaster. "I'm truly sorry you can't be here to graduate with us," writes one student. "I'm sorry that things turned out as they did," says another. A couple of her classmates report their wish that she could have stayed, and one says, "sorry we lost you so soon!" Then there are counsels of optimism: "I hope you'll be happy where you are" and, inescapably, "It always looks the darkest just before dawn." The student body president tells Mom he hopes everything will be back to normal very soon. The yearbook staff dedicates the volume "to the democracy we dearly love" and to "the inalienable rights of life, liberty, and the pursuit of happiness."

Mom got her diploma and her yearbook, but there was no way to make up the Senior Prom, which was held after the Japanese had been removed. Mom used to tell us kids how disappointed she was that she never got to wear a "long dress." Through all the years of our childhood, she never owned a formal gown. Decades later Bob, Jan, and I gave money to Mom and told her it was for a long dress. She used the money to buy a skirt and blouse. We asked her why she didn't buy a gown, and she said it wasn't practical. Timing is everything, I guess.

Maybe, though, she didn't need the prom. What was nice about Tule Lake was that it brought together—not just from Portland but from the entire Willamette Valley and Puget Sound and California and the rest of the Pacific coast—hundreds of boys, handsome Japanese boys, new boys, with whom she could go dancing. There was a dance twice, sometimes three times a week, and Mom did her best never to miss it. She even helped organize the events. There she met *yogo-res*, "hoodlums," which is what the people from the Northwest called the boys from California. The yogo-res showed her how to jitterbug. Some concentration camps are more enjoyable than others.

My father also was in camp, but four hundred miles away, at Minidoka, in southeastern Idaho. He got out of camp by volunteering for the army, which is how he got to visit Italy and France. There he got shrapnel in his shoulder that prevented him from lifting his arm over his head, and he got malaria that regularly recurred for the rest of his life and laid him low for days at a time.

While recuperating, he went back to Idaho to visit his family, who by that time had been released from camp and were working on a farm. He was still in uniform and had his arm in a sling when a white man came up and hollered, "Hey, Jap, what's the matter? Did you fall down and hurt yourself in the snow?" The inquiry was not motivated by compassion. "What are you doing in a United States army uniform?" the man continued. He then suggested that my father get out of Idaho.

It was good advice. When my father was discharged from the service with a pension for partial disability, he came to Spokane, where he met my mother. They started dating—of course they danced—and soon they married. My brother was born in 1947, my sister in 1948, and I in 1949. Baby boom boom boom. Then my father did something rare for a Japanese: he deserted his family. We went on Welfare until Mom got a job as a bookkeeper.

Growing up in the 1950s, we kids could not forget the Japanese. On our black-and-white TV, bought for us by

American Dilemmas

Uncle Hank, we watched *Bataan* and *Back to Bataan* on the late show. My brother and I read comic books that featured the devious Colonel Hakawa, he of the thick, round spectacles and buck teeth, who commanded a beleaguered garrison on some forlorn and forgotten Pacific isle. Colonel Hakawa invented diabolical weapons like the tiny booby traps he attached to ordinary balloons, as if for a birthday party, and floated in the direction of unsuspecting GIs. Despite the colonel's cleverness, his strategems never worked.

Nor could we forget that we were Japanese. One day Mom took us kids to a restaurant downtown. This must have been a special occasion, because ordinarily we couldn't afford to eat out, except at the burger joint just across the railroad tracks from our house, where they sold hamburgers for nineteen cents and gave them to you in a white paper bag with grayish yellow spots from dripping grease. No, on this day it was a real restaurant, where you sat down at a table and people waited on you.

Except they didn't. We sat for at least half an hour, maybe more. Nobody came to take our order. Eventually we got up and left. Mom said that the restaurant probably didn't serve Japanese. Of course, there's no way of knowing if that was actually the reason. Maybe some waitress just forgot which tables she was supposed to cover. You never know why you're being treated the way you are unless somebody tells you so or calls you a name. But you have suspicions.

Every few years Mom would have to go looking for a new apartment, and it was not easy. Sometimes a kindly landlady would explain that unfortunately she didn't rent to Japanese. At other times a kindly landlady—always a woman, I suppose, because the husband was away at work—would say that oh, darn it, a family had rented the apartment just a few hours earlier and she had forgotten to take down the for-rent sign. Sorry. My mother kept looking.

Mom has never owned a house, has always lived in an apartment. One summer afternoon fifteen or twenty years after I left for college, I was visiting her in Spokane, and I went to a supermarket near her home. As I was getting back into my car, I heard a woman's voice calling, "Hy-JEE-uh! Jim Hijiya, is that you?" I turned around and saw Mary, lovely Mary, on whom I had had a crush when we were in sixth and seventh and eighth grades. We chatted, and she invited me to her house nearby for "tea," which turned out actually to be lemonade. While her children played in another room, we talked of old times.

She asked me if ever, when we were young, I had been, umm, "interested" in her. I said of course I had. She said she thought so. She said that she had liked me too and that if we had gotten together back then, we could have had a lot of fun. Unfortunately, she said, she had been too prejudiced.

"Prejudiced?"

Yes, she said, back in those days she just couldn't see herself going with a Japanese.

What is the sound of one jaw dropping? When Mary and I were teen-agers, I could (and did) think of any

number of reasons why she would not want to go out with
me, which may be why I never got around to asking her
out.   However, I had not imagined that racial prejudice
would have been her reason for saying no.   She had always
been kind of me, and I had even sat at a table in the
kitchen of her house while we worked together on a
school project.   Such intercourse, however, was very
different from dating.   Once I learned about the bright
yellow line that I had been forbidden to cross, I began to
search my past for other boundaries to a prison of which I
had been unaware.

A few days after my "tea" with Mary, I had dinner
with another beautiful woman.   Kathryn was the girl I
loved most in high school, but we never went out together
until after we had left for opposite ends of the country for
college, she to Seattle and I to Providence.   Since then we
had seen each other every once in a while when in
Spokane visiting our parents.   Now, after finishing dessert,
I remembered Mary's confession.   I asked Kathryn why,
during those high school years, whenever I had asked her
out, she had always said no, she was too busy, she had to
go to a church supper or something equally compelling
instead.   Why, I asked, would she never go out with me?

"Because," she said, "you were a creep."

"Oh," I said, "I forgot."

Once when we were in college, we were walking
together in downtown Spokane.   We were stopped at an
intersection, waiting for a light, when a car full of teen-
aged boys drove by.   One of them hollered out to Kathryn:

"Hey, why don't you go with a *real* man?" She and I both pretended to ignore him.

But was it really so simple? Was it just my thick eyeglasses, my soft portliness, my shortness, my shyness, my mismatched polyester clothes, my clumsiness (no school sports, no dancing), my perfect lack of what the nineteenth century called "magnetism"? And was it just that Kathryn found my desire for her vaguely menacing, for a creep, no matter how feeble and inept, is always lurking about—creeping—stalking his prey, giving her the creeps?

Certainly these factors would have been enough to make me unattractive to girls, but were they the only reasons? Or could my creepiness have been what the logicians call "overdetermined"? Was it *also* because I was Japanese? Isn't a Jap necessarily a creep? Isn't he a monkey, rat, or snake, the feral personification of lechery and treachery? Isn't he, with his distorting glasses and sinister grin, always patiently awaiting his opportunity to molest a helpless blonde maiden or even a dark-haired but fair-skinned one? That's what Americans learned in the forties and fifties from cartoons. During the war, even the amiable Theodor Geisel, later to be known as Dr. Seuss, depicted the Japanese as round-spectacled, slant-eyed, pig-snouted, buck-toothed, grinning little demons. After the war, comic books gave us such monsters as the insidious Colonel Hakawa, and what girl would want to go out with *him*? So while I would not deny the numerous and diverse sources of my creepiness, I can't help wondering whether it stemmed in part from my being Japanese.

American Dilemmas

Well, you never know.

A few years ago a friend of mine was complaining that "minorities" were taking over the city in which she lived. "Hey!" I interrupted. "*I'm* a minority." "Oh," she replied, "but you're a *good* minority." When I was growing up, however, the Japanese had not yet become good.

My first best friend, the first I remember anyway, was Bryan. He was a Japanese boy, my age. We went to the same grade school and high school and were in the same Scout troop. We played games in the street, like Hide-and-Seek or Guns. He had a large, round magnifying glass like Sherlock Holmes's that we used, one cloudless summer's day, to make ants shrivel and smoke. We applied it to worms, too, but their writhing as their bodies blackened bothered me. It was harder to feel sympathy for something as small as an ant. It was almost a cinder already.

I envied Bryan because his mother always had a huge cylindrical metal canister filled with *kakimochi*, rice crackers flavored with soy sauce. My mom and his mom and a couple of other moms played pinochle while we boys played with model airplanes, imagining that we were shooting down our playmates. German Stuka and Jap Zero, British Spitfire, American Mustang and Flying Fortress—all swooped and veered through the bedroom air. There were even a B-52 sedately sailing and a Russian MIG bolting like a rocket through the gunfire of a war before their time. RAT-A-TAT-TAT! RAT-A-TAT-A-TAT-A-TAT-A-TAT! (That's the sound of a machine gun

67

that we learned from comic books.) POW! POW! (Fire from the cannon in a jet's nose.) Sometimes we would be interrupted by a roar of laughter from the card-players.

Bryan was the only boy in the neighborhood who was less athletic than I was. Sometimes he tried to play with us, but he never did learn to hit or catch a ball. He was small, too, even shorter than me. He was, however, very intelligent, especially proficient in math and science. Sometimes we called him "Brain," pointedly misspelling and mispronouncing his name. He also was a musician. He played piano—pronounced it pee-AH-no—and baritone horn. He and I both played baritone in the grade school band, but the difference between us was that he possessed talent. Bryan was usually first chair, while my goal at try-outs was to beat one person, anyone, so I would not be last chair. For a while I contested with Bernie, a white boy with glasses who lived so far from school that his parents had to bring him by car. (Most students walked. We had neighborhood schools in those days.) But then Bernie took private lessons, got much better than me, and became a rival of Bryan.

Bryan sometimes rubbed people the wrong way, and rubbed hard. It was as if he were trying to get even for something. Maybe it was because he was Japanese and unathletic and so short that girls couldn't see him. Who knows? But for some reason he could be combative. One snowy day after band practice, Bryan snatched the stocking cap from Bernie's head. When Bernie ran toward him, Bryan threw the cap to me. Bernie tried to get it from me, so I threw it back to Bryan. And so it went, on and on, until we reduced Bernie to a helpless, tearful fury. I am not without blame.

But at least I never humiliated a teacher. I wasn't in the class where this happened, but my cousin Dave was, and he told me about it. The teacher, perhaps the most popular one at our high school, made a point in a lecture; and Bryan said it was wrong. The teacher elaborated his argument, and Bryan systematically demolished it. Dave says the teacher never forgave Bryan, and the teacher was a very nice man.

After high school I went to college. Bryan could have gone, too—he was more than smart enough, and his parents would have paid for it. But Bryan wanted something new in his life, and he didn't want to depend on his parents. He joined the army. He tried to get into the army band but ended up instead in the infantry. I guess they needed riflemen more than baritone horn players. His mother wrote to generals and Congressmen, trying to get Bryan transferred to the band, but that did no good.

On a visit home he told me how much he hated the army. Some of his fellow soldiers called him a "gook," the same word they used for the Vietnamese. They said that when he got to Nam, he would have to be a "tunnel rat," sent down into underground hideouts to smoke out the Viet Cong. They said he was suited for it because he was so small. When the sergeants found out he was trying to get into the band, they called him "chicken," "fuck-up," and "dud." Bryan gave as good as he got. He decorated each letter to me with a large, ornate "FTA" that stood for "Fuck the Army." On a visit to the Haight-Ashbury district of San Francisco, he invested in thirty protest buttons.

Not that Bryan was entirely unmilitary—he hadn't joined the army by accident. Once he showed me a photograph of himself in battle gear, with a carbine in his hands and a ferocious grin on his round face, like the stereotypical Jap soldier in a comic book, but without the glasses. He still liked to play with guns, not altogether unlike the way we did as kids. One day when home on leave, he took a rifle out into the countryside west of town and shot at birds perched on telephone and power lines. Once he missed the bird but split the wire in two.

On the day before he shipped out for Vietnam, he wrote to me again. (All his letters are addressed to "Dear Deferred Student.") He said he was scared, and his future looked bleak. Not only were "bad guys" out to get him, but in addition he had to worry about the Viet Cong and the North Vietnamese. "Get what I mean?" he asked.

Shortly after arriving in-country, Bryan got put on what he called a "shit-burning detail," disposing of what had been deposited in the latrines at his base camp. In the movie *Jarhead*, about America's first war against Iraq, the hero gets this nasty assignment as punishment. Bryan never said why *he* was chosen for the detail, but he did tell me he didn't mind the chore too much, since at least it was something that had to be done, unlike the war itself, which he called "ridiculous." Bryan said the United States should just pull all its troops out of South Vietnam, drop ninety-six hydrogen bombs on North Vietnam, then let the

French or the Russians or the Chinese have whatever was
left.

In his first letter to me from Vietnam, he said it would
take a miracle for him to come home alive. He told me,
however, that he was not worried so much about combat
as about the eighty-pound pack he would have to carry
when he went out into the field. In his next letter, though,
after his first day away from base camp, he told me he had
nearly gotten shot by a sniper, and he did not complain
about the weight of his rucksack.

The next month, April of my freshman year at college,
I got a phone call from Western Union saying they had a
telegram for me. This was the first and last time I ever got
a telegram. The woman on the phone said she was afraid
she had some bad news, then she read the message. It was
from my mother, and I'll never forget the first sentence:
"BRYAN KILLED IN ACTION." I went outside and sat
on the lawn in front of University Hall. The sun was
shining. Some students were reading books, others
throwing Frisbees. I looked at the green grass, the red
brick building, the blue sky, and I suddenly thought that
none of it was real.

I flew home for the funeral. Bryan looked peaceful in
the coffin. His undamaged round face almost smiled. I
cried without restraint, more than at any other time I can
remember. Everybody did. Bryan's mother, Shig, was so
distraught she later was subjected to electric shock therapy.
Now she can't even remember my coming home for the
funeral, though people assure her I did.

Once, when Bryan was very young, he fell into Hangman Creek. Bryan couldn't swim, and he was drowning. Shig jumped into the deep, surging water and saved him. She couldn't swim any more than *he* could, but she wasn't going to let him die. Nobody knows how she managed to pull Bryan and herself to shore. Sometimes a mother can work miracles. There was nothing Shig could do for Bryan, though, after he joined the army.

The newspaper said that Bryan had been killed by a hand grenade, and somebody told me he had been hit in the back. Of course, a Viet Cong could have thrown it behind him, or one of Bryan's comrades might have done so by accident. Still, I've always wondered who killed him and why.

Like I said, you never know.

Forty years after Bryan's death, I looked him up on the website of the Vietnam Veterans Memorial—The Wall. The site recorded him as a "HOSTILE, GROUND CASUALTY" who had died from "MULTIPLE FRAGMENTATION WOUNDS." This was consistent with what I had heard before, though I still wasn't sure who had been hostile. It shocked me to read "Age: 19." Since I had been the same age at the time of his death, I hadn't then realized how terribly young that was—I couldn't understand it until I was much older and had lived through four decades that he had missed.

The website reported that Bryan had been male, Protestant, single. What gave me most pause, however, was another piece of information the site provided about my friend: "Race: Caucasian." Caucasian. That, I guess, was the final honor the country bestowed upon him. Posthumously, he got a promotion.

In my senior year at college I took a course on the history of Western music. Aside from one black woman and me, all the students in the class were white. One winter afternoon we went on a field trip somewhere in Connecticut to attend a performance of *Don Giovanni*. When we boarded the bus, I grabbed a window seat. (I always do. I like to look out.) The bus filled up, but nobody sat next to me. I was glad, because I like the privacy and the extra room. When all the students had boarded, I could see only one other seat still vacant, the one next to the black woman. When the professor, a white woman, got onto the bus, I wondered where she would sit. She stood next to the driver, looked about, then sat next to the black woman. Probably it was because the black woman was near the front and I was further back, or it might have been because the professor felt more comfortable seating herself next to another woman.

As the bus rolled through the countryside, I looked at the scenery streaming past. I worked on a poem; and when I got home that night, I wrote it down.

> Sunlight cold as snow
> Glitters in the bare gray boughs.
> Laughter in an empty room.

It had too many syllables for a haiku, but I figured that as a Japanese I was entitled to reformulate the rules. I named the poem "Haiku Plus Two," and it won ten dollars in a contest.

In the years since then I have noticed that when I'm on a bus or subway car filled with white people, and a black person gets on, there's a very good chance that the black person will sit next to me. *Nihonjin* and *kurombos* are not entirely different, after all.

When I was in graduate school, I played poker once in a while with other students. It was dealer's choice, and sometimes the dealer called a game named Japanese Night Baseball. I don't remember the rules—it's been a long time now—but I do recall that the game had something to do with surprise.

Graduate school was in Ithaca, New York, one of the most liberal cities in America. Still, it was in America. One day I was walking home from school, and a car filled with teen-agers drove by. They yelled "Banzai!" and threw something at me that I discovered was an apple. After the car sped away, I thought that, for everybody's sake, it was fortunate I did not carry a gun.

In my first year in Ithaca I lived in a rooming house, and one of my fellow roomers was a New Yorker named Andy. One day we were having dinner at a Chinese restaurant, and he told me his sister was a Jap. "Oh," he quickly announced, "I'd better explain. That means Jewish American Princess." Oh, I said.

Another of my housemates was named Tom Tsoy. He told me one day that he had gone to a Chinese restaurant, maybe the same one as Andy and I. The waiter asked Tom if he were Chinese. He said, no, Korean. The waiter said, that's all right, we both hate the Japanese. Tom said no, no, no, I don't hate anybody. The waiter smiled and walked away.

On the street in front of my house one day a group of urchins called me names. "Chinese Chinkee! Chinese Chinkee!" I did not bother to correct them. This was when *All in the Family* was fresh on TV, and Archie Bunker was teaching children to say "Chink." I'm sure Carroll O'Connor didn't mean to do that, but things don't always turn out as you intend.

One day, one day, one day, one day. Eventually it adds up to a life.

Don't get me wrong. I'm not saying that a white man's heaven is a Japanese hell. I like it here. Honest. Most people treat me with respect—as much, anyway, as they give to anybody. Oh, sure, when my college buddies and I were driving to Florida for spring break, there was a gas station where the attendant wouldn't let me use the bathroom, so we all got back into the car and drove on. In Fayetteville, North Carolina, we saw a billboard along the highway depicting a white-robed horseman who informed us that "This is KLAN country" and urged us to "HELP FIGHT COMMUNISM AND INTEGRATION" by joining the United Klans of America, Inc. I took a photo of my friends clowning beneath the sign. As our insouciance suggests, the Klan did not intimidate me. Of course, I never had to live in Fayetteville.

Neighbors, teachers, bosses, colleagues have been, almost without exception, not merely fair but also kind. I won't tell you that some of my best friends are white; practically all of them are. So are most of my relatives, ever since I got married. Except perhaps for a summer job digging holes for fenceposts on a dairy farm, I never got turned down for employment because I wasn't white. ("Hijiya," the farmer said, pronouncing the syllables slowly over the phone. "What kind of name is that?") No, this is not a land of oppression.

Still, ...

When I'm in a room filled with people—a living room, a concert hall, a restaurant, a classroom, a meeting—I often am the only Asian and sometimes the only person who isn't white. I'm used to that, though, so it hardly ever bothers me. In fact, I usually don't even notice it.

In America white people don't often have that experience of being alone in a crowd, alone because of the color of their skin, but they can get it by going to a foreign country and to a place not intended for tourists. My wife got it on the subway in Tokyo. It was morning rush-hour, and the car was packed with people on their way to work. We noticed that Barbara was the only person of the dozens on the car who wasn't Japanese. That is, unless you count me. Nobody said anything to her, looked at her oddly, or paid her any particular attention. Still, she told me later, she felt conspicuous and out of place.

I feel like that sometimes in the neighborhood where we live. There's a Chinese family and me, but that's about it for "people of color." When I first moved to this part of town thirty years ago, a friend told me that realtors discouraged African Americans from buying or renting houses here. I don't know whether that was true, but I do know that I still have no black neighbors.

Because I'm a racial *rara avis*, I get a lot of attention, and everybody in the neighborhood recognizes me. If they see me away from home, in the supermarket or downtown or at the university, they greet me with a hello and a handshake, real friendly. Trouble is, I sometimes don't know who they are. They're just white people, some of the hundreds I encounter every day. How am I supposed to remember who they are if they're not standing outside their house? But they all remember me.

That's one reason why I like Hawaii. Barbara and I have been there seven times, and it would be more if we could afford it. In Hawaii most of the people look like me, only thinner. I am part of the majority, profoundly inconspicuous. Sometimes people I meet there—a grocery clerk or a masseuse—will ask if I'm from Hawaii. I'll say no, what makes you think so? They'll say, oh, I don't know, you just seem like it. Maybe it's because I've learned to pronounce a few Hawaiian words or because I'm relaxed, hanging loose, when on vacation there. Or maybe it's because I'm *not* wearing a Hawaiian shirt. Whatever the reason, it's a relief to be nobody.

Martin Luther King used to say that black Americans longed for "somebodiness"—respect from other people and the self-respect that it helps to foster. If you're already "somebody," however, you usually don't even notice that you are, you don't think about it, you take it for granted. That's how I feel in Hawaii: strangely unself-conscious. I am free to become nobody, an unremarkable face in the anonymous crowd.

Chapter Four

❊ Seeing and Believing ❊

Open your eyes.
    Instead of seeing what you know is there, try to see what your eyes would see if your meddling mind did not erase what should not be there and replace it with what should. Although you know your car is gunmetal gray, allow yourself to see it as purplish brown in the bright morning light. Though you know there's a maple tree with a shapely head of red leaves shining against the sky, let yourself notice the black telephone wire slouching obstreperously in front of it. Return your eyes to innocence, like film in a camera.

Start over. If you wear glasses, take them off, as I am doing, and shut your eyes. Now open one eye—let's make it the left. Keep that right eye closed! Now, what is the shape of the world you have discovered? You may think you see everything before you, but actually your vision is defined by the tissues of your face: the eyelids, the eyebrows, even the cheekbones. We are all encased in caskets.

My left eye's field of vision is shaped like an almond, with the rounded end on the left and the pointed one on the right. At the lower right rim of that almond there is a blurry, dull wedge—my nose. If I close my left eye and open my right, the image flips over, with the sharp end of the almond now at the left and the wedge in the lower left. If I open both eyes, combining the two fields of vision, my world looks like a squat, wide rectangle, but with the corners rounded and with vague triangles cut out of the center at both top and bottom. These are the borders of my vision.

What's inside those borders is a blur, a thousand blurs—remember, I took off my glasses. I am very near-sighted. Without corrective lenses, I can read a newspaper five inches from my face, but at six it begins to get fuzzy, and at eight it's a drab gray smear. When I look around a room, I see hazily outlined dollops of various colors. Objects merge with one another and dissolve. A clock is not a round white face with black numerals punctuating its periphery but a white blob with a faint gray band along its edge. Everything is soft, it's all clouds, all I see is a chaos of colored clouds.

Then I put on my glasses. The world gets clearer but littler, or at least everything within it does. To bring a picture into focus, to project it onto the proper spot on my retina, the eyeglass lens must shrink the picture, making it appear slightly smaller than it would to a person with perfect vision. Thus, when I'm playing basketball in my driveway and standing at the free-throw line, I can see two images of the hoop: one, clearly defined, through the top section of my eyeglass lenses; and a second one, blurred, just above the eyeglass frame. The ball is as likely to drop through one as the other.

Seeing and Believing

Even in the miniaturized, precisely focused world encircled by the rims of my glasses, however, I tend to see double. I discovered this in college when I would reach for a doorknob and end up squeezing the air. My optometrist explained why that happened. Instead of cooperating to produce a single image, my eyes were operating independently, aiming in slightly different directions and producing two different images. My brain could not make sense of a twinned universe, so it would cancel out the image from the weaker eye, the left, leaving me to see only with my dominant right eye. With only one eye, however, I could not use triangulation to achieve perspective. Seeing the world in two dimensions instead of three, I had trouble calculating distance. That's why I would miss the doorknob.

The cure was exercise, and for once that tedious labor worked. At the doctor's office I would press my face against a heavy, cold, steel machine that reminded me of the viewfinder on the periscope Clark Gable and Burt Lancaster used in *Run Silent, Run Deep*. I would stare down through the eyeholes at a sheet of paper and, with a pencil in each hand, draw two converging lines, trying to make them come together to form a single straight one. This was not as exciting as shouting "Fire one! Fire two!" and sinking a Japanese freighter as the submariners did, but it was not without potential for satisfaction.

At home my equipment was simpler. The optometrist gave me a red rubber ball dangling on a strong, white string. I tacked the string's loose end to the ceiling and started the ball swinging. Then I held a prism before one eye and watched the ball. The prism moved my left eye's image of the ball so far away from my right's that my brain perceived them as totally separate phenomena and therefore did not feel compelled to abolish either of them. I would concentrate on seeing the ball through the prism, spending many minutes watching the pendulum, first with one eye, then the other. Then I would turn the prism upside down, splitting the images in a different direction, and repeat the process. While doing this, I would mitigate the boredom of my ocular calisthenics by turning on the record player and listening to the Beatles or the Mamas and the Papas.

The strategy was to strengthen the eye muscles so that I could bring the eyes under control, coordinating them to produce binocular vision. I exercised for months, hundreds of hours, following doctor's orders so scrupulously that he praised me as a model patient. I am no slave to medical authorities, but I follow their advice when it does not deprive me of my joys. I was encouraged by reading that Ted Williams in his baseball-smashing prime followed a similar regimen of eye exercise, though his objective was more exalted than mine. I kept working at it until the string slipped out of the red rubber ball and I couldn't figure how to put it back. By then, though, the ball had done its job.

I never became Ted Williams, but I did learn to see in three dimensions. For the first time in years—who knows how many?—I could clearly discriminate between one distance and another. Trees and buildings seemed to jump out at me. It was like going to one of those movies where they gave you eyeglasses with cardboard frames and one red lens and one blue one, and all of a sudden you saw the picture in 3-D. I felt like some painter of the Italian Renaissance who had just invented perspective. Wow! Look at that! My world has never been the same since.

It's work, though. It takes a conscious effort for me to keep my eyes together. When I first wake up in the morning, I see double, so I have to snap my eyes into position. All day long I have to strain to keep my vision single. Whenever I relax my eye muscles, the world immediately breaks in two. It's like being very drunk but without the dizziness.

Only recently did I learn from a book on the history of polio that diplopia, seeing double, is common among people who have had that disease. Apparently the virus that crippled the muscles in my right foot also weakened those in my eyes. The foot is connected to the eyes; there is a common thread winding through the chapters of my life; my experiences are more coherent than I had ever imagined. What weaves them all together, unfortunately, is paralysis.

My ocular machinery, then, is defective. I can't replace it, so I need repair. *Jury-rigging* might be a more accurate term. For this purpose I have a toolkit of spectacles.

Mostly I wear "progressive," "no-line" bifocals: not the Benjamin Franklin bifocals whose lenses look as if they formerly had been folded in half, but the most up-to-date type, whose uncreased lenses disingenuously deny the presence of geezer's eyes behind them. Through the top of the lenses I see objects far away; through the bottom, where the prescription is a little different, ones close up; through the center, everything in-between.

That's the theory, anyway. In practice my bifocal world, whether far or near, is almost never in perfect focus. The white lettering on green highway signs does not become legible to me until a few seconds before I reach the exit ramp, which is sometimes too late for me to change lanes. On billboards enclosing the outfield of a baseball park, I often can read the name of an advertiser but not the description of its service or product.

I have even more trouble with things within arm's reach. If I hold them far from my eyes, they are too small to see. If I hold them close, they are too blurry. This causes a problem in restaurants, especially ones whose managers believe that dim lighting is a manifestation of elegance. In such places the only way I can read the menu is to take off my glasses and hold the page five inches from my face. My burying my nose in a large, leatherbound menu, tilting it so that some precious trace of light might fall upon the print from a flickering oil lamp or a faint and distant electric bulb, causes no end of merriment for my dining companions and perhaps even for strangers at neighboring tables. When I audit the check, I sometimes confuse fives with sixes, threes with eights or even zeroes. Of course, the wine and the whiskey may have something to do with that, too.

The point is that when I know I'm going to be looking at something close up and for a long time—a book or even a newspaper—I switch to my reading glasses. When I put these on, I feel enclosed in a small space, a bubble of clarity extending only a foot from my face, because everything beyond that distance dissolves into vagueness. Even the computer monitor on my desk, two feet from my eyes, is out of focus. Therefore, a few years ago I acquired a third set of glasses, for use solely when I am tapping at the keyboard and bullying a mouse across the desk.

When I'm working at my desk, it is cluttered with eyewear. At my left, next to the telephone, are my regular glasses, the no-line bifocals. In front of me, on the stand that supports the iMac screen, lie my computer glasses. To my right, near the plastic coaster that sometimes holds my glass of bourbon and sometimes weighs down loose papers, I keep my reading glasses.

As I read a manuscript, scribble corrections in the margins, type those corrections into the computer, print hard copy, get up and go to the bathroom while the printer hums and whirs, then come back and sit down to read the revised version, I have to change my glasses again and again. Sometimes, amidst the stacks of paper and books on my desk, I misplace a pair of glasses, pick up the wrong ones, and put them on. For a few seconds I struggle to see, then eventually discover my error. When I then search for the proper eyewear, I have to look closely to discern which of the two pairs reposing on the desk is it. Such confusion troubles my tidy soul, but I have learned that for some ills in life there is no remedy.

I got my first pair of glasses in grade school; my mother tells me I was having trouble seeing the blackboard. I can date the year of acquisition from class pictures. In second grade my face is uncovered and surprisingly cute—surprising to me now, that is. By third grade, however, black-rimmed spectacles, slightly cockeyed, tilted down to my left, have transformed the face into one that is recognizably mine.

In my senior year of college I tried to get cute again: I bought contact lenses. The optometrist warned me that I should start by wearing them just a few hours each day, then slowly increase the duration. Such gradualism, however, proved both unnecessary and impossible—unnecessary because once I got the lenses in, I could wear them all day without discomfort; impossible because it took me practically all day to get them in.

I have a phobia about my eyes. I can't stand putting anything into or even near them. I would place the contact lens onto the tip of my right forefinger, then, using the fingertips of my left hand to pry apart the lids of an eye, try to inject the contact. Almost invariably I would fail. Some unseen force would arrest my fingertip half an inch from my eyeball. I would will the finger forward, the straining hand and arm would go rigid, and the biceps would form a premonition of a bulge; yet still that invisible force would hold the finger back until a pressure built up between the fingertip and the eye that was volcanic. Finally and suddenly the resistance would collapse, and my finger would jolt forward, stabbing my eyeball and sending my head reeling back, the contact lens glancing off somewhere onto the table or floor. I would wash it off and try again. Eventually I would get the contact in, but then I still had to contend with the other eye.

Everybody told me that in time I would grow accustomed to inserting my lenses. Everybody was wrong. After a month the process was still averaging two hours a day. I had books to read and classes to attend, and I couldn't afford to spend two hours assembling my eyes. Therefore, I returned to glasses. I still have the contact lenses in a handy plastic carrying case in a cardboard box in the basement. They have turned the color of bourbon.

For years people told me I should try contacts again. They're better now, softer, easier to put in—that's what everybody said. I did not repeat my folly, however. Physics and engineering, medicine and psychology—all these together are still no match for panic.

I also have glaucoma. In most patients this disease reveals itself through uncommonly great pressure created by the aqueous humor, the fluid inside the eyes. In *my* eyes, however, the pressure was within the normal range (albeit at the upper end of it), so my ophthalmologist could diagnose the disease only by using a powerful microscope that detected a fraying of the optic nerve of my right eye. This "Normal Tension Glaucoma" is common among people of Japanese descent—not Chinese or Korean, just Japanese—almost like a national disease. The standard therapy for this condition is to reduce eye pressure, in the hope that this will prevent or at least retard further deterioration.

For a couple years I tried to do this by squeezing drops of medicine from little plastic bottles into each eye every morning and night. I applied first one kind of eyedrop, then another, then two or three kinds in various combinations. This lowered the pressure in my eyes, but not enough. When a series of "visual field tests" revealed the appearance and expansion of sectors in my field of vision where images were fuzzy and faint, despite the river of medicine I had poured into that eye one drop at a time, my doctor decided it was time to operate.

First he used a laser to puncture tiny holes in the surface of the eye so that excess fluid could escape. That made no difference.

Then he performed a surgery called a "trabeculectomy" that cut a tiny "trapdoor" (his term) in the eye. Aqueous humor now flows out the trapdoor and into a "bleb," a little, bubble-shaped reservoir the surgeon created on the white of the eye, above the pupil but hidden by my eyelid. From there the fluid gradually dissolves and disperses through the capillaries. To push the fluid out of my eyeball and into the bleb, I "massage" my eye three times a day, pressing my right forefinger against the bottom of my eye for five seconds. To me this procedure seems crudely, almost comically, mechanical, but it also seems to work. After I massage my eye, the pressure in it falls below the normal range, at least for a few hours.

Such success, however, has not stopped the advance of glaucoma. Slowly, haltingly, but with seeming inexorability, my blind spots have continued to expand, and the blindness within each one has grown more complete. Sometimes I take off my glasses, thinking the right lens has gotten smudged around the edges, but I discover that the lens is spotless. It is my vision itself that has gotten smudged. If I bob my head up and down and turn it from side to side, I can find a position that enables my right eye to perceive an object with a tolerable degree of clarity. Much of what surrounds that object, however, is a blur. Were it not for my healthy left eye, I would have a hard time driving a car or reading a book.

When the opthalmologist first detected my glaucoma, I had not yet noticed its effects: my visual field was as expansive and clear as ever. Now, however, the impairment is severe enough that I can't help but notice it: I can see that I can't see. If the deterioration of my vision continues, I suppose that eventually my right eye will become effectively, legally, appallingly blind. This used to be my stronger, dominant eye, the one on which I mainly relied.

My doctor tells me that if a person has glaucoma in one eye, there is a better than average chance that sooner or later he will develop it in the other. This is one of those tidbits of medical information about which I try not to think. I remain hopeful that I'll never go blind in both eyes. With luck, I'll die first. After that, I won't mind having eyes that do not see.

When I was young, I read William Blake's assertion that the eyes are the windows of the soul. That made sense to me, but I misunderstood. I thought the poet meant that if you looked deeply into somebody's eyes, you could see his—or, since this interested me more, her—soul. I wanted to look at girls, pretty girls, and see who they really were. I wanted to be a spiritual Peeping Tom.

Of course I couldn't do that. When I placed myself in front of a girl and tried to fix my eyes on hers, my glance would bounce away like a peewee marble off a boulder. Maybe it was because, as a Japanese, I had been trained to regard a stare as a form of attack: I swear that two Japanese could spend a whole day together and never come face to face for more than a second. But probably it's just me. I don't like to look people in the eye, implying that I'm telling the truth and testing whether they are. I hate such demonstrations of sincerity. Therefore, I was never able to peer through the windows at anyone's naked soul.

Decades later I discovered I had been looking in the wrong direction. What Blake actually said was that the soul looks out through (not with) the eyes to perceive the heavens. I had been looking for somebody else's soul, when my soul should have been looking for reality. So many years wasted! I am a fool.

Not entirely wasted, though, not always. My literary scholarship may have been as misshapen as my eyeballs, but nonetheless I sometimes managed to see. I just had to look at something other than girls.

One summer when I was in high school, my friend Art and I went camping on Mount Rainier, the loftiest peak in the Cascade Range (south of Canada, that is). We wanted to drive ourselves, but my mother didn't trust teen-agers alone in a car on winding mountain roads. At her

90

insistence, and with my furious resentment after a long argument, I consented to allow Art's dad to drop us off at the end of the road, at a place called Paradise. From there Art and I hiked up almost to the timberline—higher than Paradise!—and set up camp off the trail and near the base of a tall waterfall. The stream of meltwater, glacier turned liquid, crashed a hundred feet away.

That night was so cold the water froze in our canteens and in the steel bucket we kept next to the campfire. The next day, however, was sunny and hot. We climbed up onto the glacier and played. How strange to be shirtless and sweating, with snow and ice beneath our feet! Once, I looked down and saw, through a sheet of translucent ice, a torrent of water rushing beneath me. I wondered what would happen if the ice should crack open and I plunge in. Would I shoot a few minutes later over the waterfall by our camp and come to rest lodged against a granite boulder amidst leafless broken branches in the stream? Or would I sink to the bottom of the glacier and be found ten thousand years later to the astonishment and delight of archaeologists? I tucked away that thought for later rumination.

Art and I were wearing sneakers. We would hike up to a high ridge on the glacier, find a slope of ice, run down it, then brace our legs and slide as far as we could. We did it again and again. After one particularly exhilarating slide of a dozen yards or more, I ambled a few feet further down the slope before starting another run, taking time to catch my breath. I found myself at the edge of a cliff, maybe a hundred feet straight down, though it looked to

91

me like a thousand. I was glad my last slide had ended when, and how, it did. I thought that maybe my mother was right after all: children should not play on mountains.

But I have forgotten to tell you of my vision!

One evening during this campout—the first evening, I believe, though the word *evening* is misleading, since it suggests the onset of darkness, and the sun was still well above the horizon, though the hour was late—Art and I stood in a clearing and watched the clouds roll up. Not in—*up*. We were so high on the mountain that we could look down and see the clouds gather below like invading armies. Then, as time passed, they marched up the slope. We watched, fascinated, as they inexorably approached. Then, so gradually we hardly noticed when it happened, they enveloped us. The world became gray and soft, and I realized for the first time—I was only sixteen, and I had never flown in an airplane—that fog was just a cloud that was all around you instead of up in the sky where it belonged. Now, as the world went dim, Art was gone, the tent was gone, the mountain was gone, everything was gone.

Except the waterfall. I looked up and saw the magnificent silver river, leaping out of the gray cloud above me, pouring down radiantly through the air, and disappearing again into the drab, devouring cloud below. I discovered the difference between silver and gray. The eruption was a fish jumping from the water, an illumination, almost a revelation. I don't know how long I stood there watching. I said to myself, "God is taking a piss," and the thought was not entirely sacrilegious.

A few days later we hiked down the mountain without incident. Art's father picked us up at Paradise and drove us home.

The next time I had an epiphany like the one with the waterfall was after a Winter Mixer in graduate school. A mixer for people in their twenties or thirties is bound to be a sad affair. For two or three hours I stood around a punch bowl with the rest of the guys. It was just like a high school mixer except that the punch was laced with brandy and rum. Meanwhile, half the women in attendance—the fortunate few—were gaily frantic with men's attention, while the other half had plunged into sullen despair. All this to the noise of the latest rock and roll. My own attitude was one of resignation. I was not surprised that no woman attempted to seduce me. Eventually I gave up and prepared to walk down the hill, to a house I shared with four other men. At the top of the hill, however, I stopped and looked.

Stars all across the sky! Snow, beautiful sweet white snow, quietly covering the slopes of the hills, the rooftops in the valley below, the shores of the vast, frozen lake; covering, it seemed, the entire world. The night was white and bright as the moon. I stared with my mouth open but wordless. I don't know how long that lasted. Eventually I walked down the hill to my house, paying no attention to my footing in the slippery snow. Maybe I fell down a time or two, who could tell? In the warmth of home I threw off my clothes and hurled myself onto the mattress on the floor of my second-story room with its low, sloped ceiling, alone as usual.

I was happy beyond belief. This is what it means to see.

I have not had many such visions since then. They were, for me, a privilege of youth. But even now, in these later days, I often have sights that remind me of what I have seen before.

This is why I walk—not because I enjoy the exercise but because it gives me an opportunity to see. In this my priorities differ from those of my wife, Barbara. When we go for a walk, she seeks to maximize its aerobic benefits by stepping fast, forcing the lungs to pump, stressing the body to make it stronger. I dawdle and lag behind, slowing to a snail's pace so I might notice, say, an edible berry or leaf. It is not every walker who has learned to emulate the snail. Barbara communes with her cell phone while waiting for me to catch up.

The slowest walk I remember was once during college when I was camping alone. I went to fill a pail with river water that in those days I thought fit to drink, despite the cattle that meandered through it. I looked about me and appreciated everything: the battling blue and white stream, the gleaming rocks along its banks, the bold sun. It was on camping trips like these that deer wandered past my tent and glanced at me as I glanced at them, curious and unafraid. On these excursions I ate macrobiotics—brown rice, apples, green tea—and the deer seemed to think I was as harmless as themselves.

On this particular bright morning, as I walked to the river, filled a canvas pail, and returned to the tent, I felt impervious to time. Every step I took seemed like the entirety of my life. When I finally got back to camp, I glanced at my wrist—I'm surprised I was still wearing my watch, though I suppose it is an indelible stamp of my devotion to the precisely measured and demarcated life—and I discovered that to traverse, round trip, the hundred yards between my camp and the river, I had spent an hour and a half. Where did the time go? Where did I?

I still take long walks, mostly on Cape Cod these days, on the blank beaches of winter, over the parabolic sand hills, through the little wildernesses of pitch pine and beach plum. In a desert like this there is much to observe. Thomas Edison once said that the body is a machine for carrying the brain around, but I am no Edison. For me the body is a machine for carrying the eyes.

The peregrine, weighing a pound and a half, has eyes bigger than a man's; eyes heavier than its brain. Birds, of course, are not exactly famous for their intellect. Still, I would not mind being the drifting falcon whose enormous eyes detect the dove plodding through the thick air far below, entirely unaware of the disaster about to befall it at two hundred miles an hour. The peregrine is very good at judging distances.

Sometimes I stand nervously atop a sandy cliff overlooking the Atlantic and focus my binoculars on a flotilla of red-breasted mergansers or buffleheads. At other times, I take a field guide from my pants pocket and, looking down at flowers on the side of a trail, try to distinguish one from another. This is where my near-sightedness can be an advantage. If I have to examine something tiny—for example, the styles at the center of a campion blossom, to determine whether it's a bladder campion (three styles) or a white one (five)—I take off my glasses and pull the flower within four inches of my left eye. It's like using a magnifying glass. People with normal vision can't seen anything clearly that close-up, but for me it's easy. I make the most of my myopia.

It is intellectually satisfying to identify wildflowers, especially the tiny ones you might crush beneath your feet without even noticing them—blue-eyed grass, maiden pink, heal-all. However, it is a *palpable* pleasure to crunch glasswort (sea salt between your teeth) or feel the bite of poor man's pepper on the back of your tongue even after you have swallowed the seeds. And who would have thought that common milkweed had such a sweet smell? Or how much fun it would be to squeeze the seed pod of touch-me-not and feel it explode in the palm of your hand? However, you would not be able to enjoy plants this way if you did not see them first—if you did not, that is, *look*.

Each morning that the weather and the clock permit, Barbara and I walk about our neighborhood. Sometimes we go to the harbor and take a peek at the water lapping the piers, to see how high the tide is. At the marsh we admire the egrets' gangly grace; and as we start for home, we step around the green goose droppings at the boat landing where a well-intentioned woman scatters clumps of stale bread. On some of our walks we go the other way, to the sandy beach where we swim in the summer, and look for ducks, cormorants, and, in the warmer months, shore-scuttling peeps. Sometimes we walk down High Street to the gated mansions at the end and walk back. Sometimes we go around and around our house in widening rectangles.

We see the construction in our neighborhood: new houses going up, old ones being remodeled and enlarged. We see people going somewhere, driving, jogging, walking like us, walking the dog, going out in their bathrobes to pick the newspaper off the dewy lawn. We say good morning and wave. If we're lucky, we hear a mockingbird's raucous recital or see its white-dappled wings flash by. Once we watched half a dozen brazen cardinals fling themselves one by one across the street. On rare occasions we see deer browsing on tulips in flower beds, and we wonder where they sleep at night. There aren't many empty spaces left.

One morning many years ago when I was in college, on my way to class, I saw a woman a block ahead of me, meandering back and forth across the sidewalk. Because I was walking straight and fast, driven by conscientious purpose, I quickly caught up with her and discovered that it was someone from my music history class. She and I were both seniors; but she was a music major, a flutist, and I always wondered why she was in the introductory class. I supposed it was just because it was required for her major and she had never gotten around to taking it before. She was a very pretty woman and of a social class higher than mine; a library on campus was named after one of her ancestors. That's what I had heard, anyway. At least she had the same last name as the library. One day she got behind me in line at a supermarket. I said hello, but she did not reply. Probably she didn't hear me or didn't realize I was talking to her; but, just in case she was ignoring me, I did not repeat my greeting.

On this later morning, however, as she shuttled across the sidewalk, dodging mud puddles, looking up at the gray sky and down at the pavement, observing the stone steps and dark doorways and clapboard walls of old buildings, I felt empowered, inspired, to speak to her. "What are you doing?" I asked. "Why are you going back and forth?"

She looked at me with eyes bright with surprise, and she spoke in a voice that was childlike and soft. "Because," she said, "there's so much to *see!*"

Those were her first and last words to me. I nodded and walked on. When I heard of her again—read about her, actually—she had made her debut at Carnegie Hall.

Have you ever noticed how much you can see with your eyes closed? Maybe this is what it looks like when you're blind.

If I'm on my back at the beach, lying on a straw mat, with my face to my beloved sun but my eyes shut tight, I see sheets of red, purple, yellow, orange, white, in different shades of every color. The hues come, I suppose, from the tissues and fluids in my eyelids as the sun shines through them (the skin is thinner on the eyelids than anywhere else on the body). I also see a few dark, wriggly lines, like rivers on a map, that slowly rise and fall. I don't know what these are, but they may be blood vessels. What gives them the illusion of motion is my eyeballs' rolling up and down behind the lids, making the lines seem to move in the opposite direction.

I also have much to watch at night. When I close my eyes in bed, I do not see just the darkness. If I pay attention, I see embedded in that vast field of black a galaxy of tiny spots of light in many colors. These are not the flashes of light my ophthalmologist has warned me about, the sudden, bright explosions of color that signify I should rush to his office because my retina, strained by the excessive curvature of my myopic eye, is peeling off in strips like old wallpaper from the concave back of my eyeball. Nor is this the terrible fireworks I heard about in El Salvador from a man who had been tortured by the security forces. They put a sheet of heavy plastic over his head and tied it around his neck to form what they called *la capucha*, the hood. They filled the hood with powdered lime, the white stuff you spread on your yellowing lawn to turn it green, then pounded him on the back and punched him in the stomach so that, willy-nilly, he had to inhale deeply, sucking the lime into his lungs, which sent a brilliant shower of colors flashing through his brain. He told me he had never imagined there were so many colors in the world.

No, no, the colors I see are infinitely more benign than that, an uncountable multitude of microscopic lights, quiet and serene. There is, of course, an enormous background of black; but emerging from that background, or maybe merging with it, are those millions of little lights, blending together to form a spectacular tapestry of color. I suppose that if you could see all the stars in the night sky above you, even those too many millions of light-years away for the most powerful telescope to detect, and if you could see all those stars in the full spectrum of colors, it would present a scene like this, a vision of the universe.

This is what I see, anyway, in the dark. Maybe it's just my imagination, but maybe not.

Shut your eyes and look. You might be amazed by what you see.

Chapter Five

❊ Eat, Drink, and Be ❊

I have a small mouth. I did not say *quiet* or *inactive*, as if to deny possessing what is derided as a "big mouth"; I said *small*. My meaning is merely literal.

I have heard that a large mouth is a sign of good-heartedness, generosity, joviality—a great dark cave filled with laughter. I have found that to be true, sometimes, in women. I would like to believe, however, that the minuteness of my mouth does not betoken a meanness of spirit.

In any event, my mouth has proven large enough to provide me with sustenance and pleasure. What more can you ask of a hole in your face?

Because my mouth is small, the dentist and hygienist have their work cut out for them. I open as wide as I can, but they still have little room in which to operate. When they have to take an X ray, clamping what looks and feels like a photographic slide between a tooth and my esophagus, they sometimes need two or three attempts before they can get the cardboard rectangle into place.

Here, though, it's not principally the smallness of my mouth that's to blame but, rather, my "gag reflex." Like my eyes, my throat won't tolerate being touched. Whether it's the physician's oversized Popsicle stick or the dentist's little round mirror at the end of a silver pole, whenever something threatens to choke me, panic sets in.

Because of my propensity to choke and gag, to fight back furiously against any invasion of the sacred homeland of my mouth, my dentist used to sedate me with laughing gas. First he would place a rubber mask over my nose to administer the nitrous oxide, which relaxed me and made it possible for him to thrust his fist inside my mouth and jab me with a needle filled with Novocain. Only after the latter drug had taken effect, usually after a second injection, would he begin to fill the cavity in my tooth. In the meantime I could enjoy the elation produced by the gas. I don't remember ever actually laughing, but the drug made me happy, made me smile. It also made it possible for the dentist to choke and stab me.

Sometimes, though, there were complications. Once, as I sat ensconced in the dentist's reclining chair, waiting for the Novocain to numb my mouth, I was reading a paperback book when suddenly I had a revelation. I realized that what I was doing—holding the book in my hands, waiting for the dentist to return, thinking these thoughts—I had done a thousand or a million times before. Eternal Recurrence! The same event happening over and over, exactly the same, forever and ever; my whole life, the whole history of the universe, repeating itself indefinitely—and I had figured it out!

The dentist came back into the room and gave me a second shot. But of course he had done that an infinite number of times before, and the words he spoke to me were exactly the ones he had used all the other times. When he left the room again, I, with a mixture of excitement and horror, turned my book to a blank page in back and, in vivid detail, recorded all my discoveries, filling the entire page and part of the next. "THIS IS HELL," I wrote. "Round and round."

I thought, though, that if only I could remember what I had learned, if I could establish a point of view outside the incessant cycle, I could break free of it, stop the wheel's endless spin. That's why I was writing in the book: to remind myself, to preserve evidence, to have proof. With the notes in my book I could teach the world the truth, I could free mankind from its entrapment in endless repetition. I would be a *boddhisattva*, someone who has achieved enlightenment but who, out of kindness, forgoes nirvana and instead remains in the world to show others how to escape the sticky coils of birth and rebirth.

But then something terrible happened, something frightening. I fell asleep.

When I awoke, the dentist and his assistant were looking down at me, putting clamps on my mouth, getting ready to operate. I looked at my lap and saw the book still open to the pages on which I had written. I realized that They must have read it: They knew that I knew what was happening. They would not want me to escape and tell the world. They would destroy my book. What would They do to me? What would They *not* do?

I wanted to rip everything out of my mouth—the steel and the plastic, the gauze and the rubber—all of it.   I wanted to jump from the chair and flee, escape from

Them. But I knew They wouldn't let me. I realized I had to stay calm, act nonchalant, as if nothing had happened. I casually closed the book and talked politely of the trivial. They poked and scraped; drilled, packed, and rinsed; just as They always did. Yes, yes, yes, my plan was working. Maybe They hadn't even looked in my book at all. How careless of the fools!

By the time they were done, the laughing gas had worn off. I was back to normal, or as normal as I ever am. I drove home. When I got there, I opened my book to the fatal page and noted the very first message I had written to myself that day: "Don't stop the gas! This stuff ought to be illegal, it's so much fun."

As it turned out, I didn't stop the gas; the government did. The state legislature passed a law making it almost impossible for dentists to use nitrous oxide anymore. Since then I've had to struggle with my nerves, my gagging, my fears. Sometimes they're so bad the dentist has to skip a procedure. Sometimes I have to come back another day and try again.

Maybe it's just as well.

There's a dream I've had three or four times, maybe half a dozen, about my teeth. One of them, a canine, is loose. I grab it between a thumb and forefinger and wiggle it. With hardly a tug, I pull it out. Then I notice another tooth is loose, so I pull it out, too. Then another and another until my mouth is half empty.

I know that by telling this story I provide grist for the Freudians' mill. They think that everything is a symbol of sex. I am more inclined to believe that sex is a symbol of everything.

In this particular fiction, however, there is no symbolism: the dream about teeth is just about teeth or, to be more exact, the absence of teeth. My mother has some false teeth, and she finds them troublesome. Sometimes when eating she covers her mouth with her hand. She's not the only one with problems like that. My Uncle Hank used to take his false teeth out when he ate, they were so cumbersome. In his final years, he didn't wear them at all. After my friend Ed's father got his last remaining teeth pulled to make way for a full set of dentures, he proclaimed to his family: "Thunuvabith. Thunuva*bith*! If feelth yike eye gah a mowfulla *thyit* !" I do not look forward to losing teeth.

What gives wings to my nightmare is not just fear of the future but also memory of the past. I remember losing my baby teeth: the pain and the blood and the caves in my gums. My mother washed each ejected tooth and placed it in a glass of water on my nightstand. The next morning the tooth was gone, and a dime was in its place, the shiny cash assuaging the trauma of losing a part of my body. I think the loss of baby teeth is a premonition of old age, when the corporeal machine breaks down one piece at a time until, finally, the creaking contraption suddenly and entirely ceases to run.

In the meantime I do all I can to keep my teeth. I brush after each meal—I used to be the only one carrying a toothbrush and paste into the men's room at the university—and I floss before I go to bed. I massage my gums with a rubber pick, and I use a toothpaste that has so much fluoride it requires a prescription. I get the best of care from a dentist, a periodontist, an endodontist, and an oral surgeon. If I fail to keep my mouth intact, it won't be for lack of trying.

The main reason for having teeth, of course, is to eat. Not for a moment have I forgotten this fundamental fact.

I love to eat. Long ago I read a book of wisdom that said you ought to eat to live, not live to eat. My priorities, however, are exactly the opposite. We are on this earth for a brief time only, and much of that time is filled with sorrow and pain, so why should we not make the most of what gives us pleasure? And what source of pleasure is more abundant and convenient than food? Friends can be false, lovers fickle, dogs may turn around and bite you, but you can always count on food. It doesn't change, and it's always there for you.

My mother used to make split pea soup, chili, fried chicken, rainbow trout caught by my Uncle Fred, and fresh corn from the garden, tossed into the house through the living room window. We had commonplace Japanese dishes like sukiyaki and teriyaki but also ones you can't get in a restaurant, like hamburger-and-cabbage, seasoned with soy sauce. We always had turkey for both Thanksgiving and Christmas because my brother Bob or I or both of us would have a paper route, and the newspaper company gave turkeys to its carriers on those holidays. When Bob and I both had routes at the same time, we would have one turkey left over to give to neighbors. I didn't know it was possible to have anything *but* turkey on Thanksgiving or Christmas.

Unlike advocates of health and ecology, I have never scorned "prepared" foods. On the contrary, I have a powerful nostalgia for certain "packaged" foods that once delighted me but now are no longer on the market, like Campbell's Chili Beef soup or Rice-a-Roni's Rice Provence (we pronounced it "Rice Province"). Fortunately, my all-time favorite "comfort food"—what I eat to cheer myself, calm myself, remind myself that the world is not as bad as it seems at the moment—still comes in a green cardboard box labeled "Kraft Tangy Italian Spaghetti Classics." It's not as tangy as it used to be—less garlicky, I believe. My mother used to say that when my brother and I ate it, she could smell it on our breath for days. Maybe that's why we liked it so much we sometimes ate it for breakfast. Since then, the sauce has gotten blander, and the spaghetti has become hard to find in stores, so I sometimes have to resort to ordering it online, direct from the company. It's worth it. Sometimes, when I have insomnia, I'll drink beer and eat Kraft Spaghetti. If that won't help me fall asleep at four in the morning, I don't know what will.

Around the age of nine, I got into the habit of eating a snack after I got home from school, to tide me over until dinner. There was an ice cream truck that parked by the school playground; and if I had money, I would buy a pineapple milkshake or a banana split. I grew so chubby that my linguistically inventive brother described me as "protuberant" or even "porculent." I grew thinner in high school, as I grew taller; but in college, when I ceased to gain altitude, I resumed my progress toward rotundity.

I learned many things in college, not least important of which were exotic cuisines. I found that a Chinese meal didn't have to include chow mein; I discovered the provinces of Szechuan and Hunan. My pal Szymanoski introduced me to kielbasa, pierogis, and golabkis, and taught me to pronounce the last one "go-WUMP-kees." I found that a good cut of steak should not be cooked to death. Of course, when I was a kid, we never *had* a good cut of steak, so the texture didn't matter much. Why do they call dried-out beef "*well*-done," anyway?

My first three years in college I lived on campus and ate at the "Ratty," the refectory. Everybody complained about the food, but I thought it was fine. You could go back for seconds or thirds—what more could you want? There also was a food truck that parked every night outside the dorm, and we would interrupt our study or card playing to fetch a cheeseburger "grinder": an elongated hamburger with lots of creamy cheese on a toasted roll. I never found a restaurant making a grinder as good, nor could I duplicate it at home. Some nights we would drive downtown to a trailer parked out front of Providence City Hall, where we would order a "bowl of reds with one cut up." That was our slang for kidney beans with a chopped hot dog added. That trailer is still there at night, when the drunks get hungry, but the truck doesn't serve beans anymore. Tastes have changed.

It was in college that I acquired the nickname "The Bottomless Pit." This referred to my eating habits: my friends would observe my gargantuan performance, astounded and aghast. Even now I sometimes consume enough to startle witnesses. A few years ago at a baseball game in Los Angeles I amazed my nephew by eating Dodger Dogs *and* enchiladas—I could not pass up either of the local specialties—as well as the peanuts and ice cream I could get at any ballpark in the country. And that was just a snack between meals.

Nevertheless, I don't eat as much as formerly. At home I sometimes will have only one large plate of pot roast or lasagna instead of two or three, and from a restaurant I will often take away a covered styrofoam bowl of leftovers. This is not because I have grown wise and have learned to discipline myself, depriving myself of pleasurable degustation now in order to secure long life, good health, and a trim physique in the future. No, it is just because I am not as hungry as I used to be.

I still am a slave to my body. If it says, "Eat," I do. But if it says, "Stop," I obey. Either way, I follow the Pleasure Principle. It is, after all, a principle.

Of course, I am pudgy: my belly hangs over my belt. If most people ate as much as I do, however, they would weigh three hundred pounds. I must be blessed with a fast metabolism.

I am not, however, a fast eater. I chew my food a long time, then let it sit on my tongue and slide about my mouth before I swallow. Before taking another bite, I think about the previous one, remembering how tasty it was. Poor Richard said that "appetite is the best sauce," but I think the crucial ingredient is memory. I'm almost always the last one at the table to finish eating. The only exception is when I'm with my mother, who has always eaten more languidly than I, even when she had all her teeth. Maybe I learned slow eating from her.

It bothers me to see people eat fast. They never lay down their forks, as if doing so would cost them valuable time. They pitch food into their mouths so rapidly, so continuously, that I think I am in a factory. And yet they say they enjoyed the food—"Loved it! Delicious!" But the way they ate it, I don't see how they could possibly have even noticed what it was.

Of course, that's just me. I'm a slow reader, too. If the writing is good, I want to savor it, not rush past. People make fun of you if you move your lips when you read, but how else can you taste the words? So please forgive me if I take the time to move my jaws while I eat.

I can't imagine not enjoying food, but I know for a fact that some people don't. Once I asked a pretty young woman out to lunch. As we dined, she told me she didn't like to eat: she wished somebody would invent a pill with all the necessary nutrients so she wouldn't have to waste time eating. I asked her what she did enjoy doing. She said sunbathing. I asked if she read books while doing that. She said no, she just basked in the sun. I did not ask her out again. Even I have *some* requirements.

Lobster, prime rib (rare) au jus with horseradish, clams and oysters on the half shell, pasta bolognese—these are a few of my favorite things. You can keep the schnitzel with noodles. In the morning sometimes I'll revert to my "bachelor's breakfast" of coffee and potato chips. Salted peanuts or deep-fried cheese curls may be substituted for the chips. I drink my coffee black in order to control my intake of calories and cholesterol.

You'll notice the absence of vegetables, whose usual blandness allows me to consume them but does not make me eager to do so. If I have a choice between soup and salad, I'll take the soup, unless it's minestrone or the salad is shrimp or crab or Caesar at least: Parmesan cheese and anchovies can make me forget I'm eating lettuce. I know, however, that vegetables provide my body with vitamins and fiber it needs, so I accept vegetables as a kind of medicine. I eat them with the same dutiful resolve with which I swallow a pill: no pain, but also no pleasure.

My favorite juice is grapefruit juice, and I drank it every day until I read that it could kill me. Supposedly grapefruit juice prevents the body from absorbing simvastatin, the drug I take to lower my cholesterol, causing the drug to accumulate in the liver in quantities that can be fatal. After pondering this possibility, I started drinking the juice only four times a week, instead of every day, and always in the morning, thus erecting a barrier of time between it and the simvastatin I take at night. I refuse to give up the juice entirely, however. Not only is it one of the few sources of Vitamin C that tastes good to me, but also, if someday I die of liver disease, I want people to say that it was the grapefruit juice that did me in.

Maybe I'm too much of a carnivore: I am a great eater of beef. When I was teaching, I would sometimes invite my seminar students to dinner. One year they were surprised to discover no beans in my chili. I had to explain that the dish is named chili con carne, not chili con frijoles. Another year I served spaghetti, and one student told me I had given her an entirely new idea of meat sauce: not sauce with meat, but meat with sauce.

I understand why some people don't eat meat. It's cruel to kill animals, especially since I could get my fill of protein from tofu and bean sprouts instead. In order to provide beef for my plate, the average steer probably consumes the grass and water of an area the size of Rhode Island, while burping and farting enough methane to raise the temperature of Earth's atmosphere by half a degree, Celsius. In the vegetarian future, people will probably look back on meat-eating with the same horror and amazement with which we now regard slavery or the burning of heretics. Nevertheless, I obstinately eat what tastes good to me, what makes me happy. I probably won't stop devouring flesh until I survive my first heart attack. Or don't.

My doctors do not recommend the kinds of food I prefer, especially in view of my naturally high counts of blood sugar and cholesterol. I don't worry much, though—there are pills I take to lower those statistics. Montaigne, even though he lived before such convenient pharmaceuticals were invented, said he was always harmed by foods that tasted bad, but never by any he swallowed joyfully. Even Seneca, the Stoic, declared that only a fool would entirely sacrifice the pleasures of the present in order to preserve inviolate his hopes of the future. These sages of old are my most trusted physicians.

Eat, Drink , and Be

When I go to a restaurant for dinner, I begin with two cocktails—*two* because I have found that the second one is often better than the first, "better" meaning heavier on the booze. I think this is because bartenders know that anybody having a second whiskey is serious about drinking. Such a customer doesn't order a drink just because everyone else is doing so.

Another reason for the second cocktail is that a solo one has no effect on me and therefore is a waste. Only while savoring that second drink do I begin to find the world transformed. The food becomes tastier, the people around me more attractive, their conversation more intriguing, whether I can hear it over the din of the restaurant or not. My own stories get better as well. Some people have told me they can achieve this extra intensity of experience through a philosophical change of attitude, without resorting to alcohol, and I suppose they can. However, they remind me of the Christian Scientist who told me that if I had faith, I would not need eyeglasses. Lacking both faith and philosophy, I make do with bifocals and bourbon.

Moralists deplore using liquor to evade problems instead of confronting them, but what if the problems are insoluble? Many years ago a woman I loved would not speak to me on the telephone, so I drank tumbler after tumbler of bourbon and soda while listening to blues on the stereo. At a certain moment in the black center of the night, I thought it would be amusing to explode the whiskey glass against the wall of my apartment. I hurled the glass, but it did not break. The wall broke. I had opened a hole in the painted plaster above the television. When I walked over to inspect the damage, I stepped on a wire connecting the record player to a speaker, snapping the wire and turning the stereo into monaural. After that I went to bed.

The next morning I had a hangover. I dropped off the record player at a repair shop, then went to a hardware store for plaster, paint, and wire mesh. I had never plugged a hole in a wall before. The hardware salesman—a former student of mine—told me how to do it, and he even came to my house to help me; but the project took all day. I did not think much about the woman who would not talk to me. That's what alcohol can do for you: turn a heartache into a headache—something more manageable.

I remember my first whiskey, Vat 69, an inexpensive scotch. I was only sixteen, so my mother got it for me—if you knew my mother, you would not be surprised. My brother was home on leave from the navy, and he and I wanted to get drunk, but neither of us was old enough to gain admittance to the Washington State Liquor Control Board retail outlet. We presented our dilemma to Mom, and she said she would buy the booze if we would pay for it. We did, and she did. While Mom was in the liquor store, Bob and I waited nervously in the parking lot, like drivers of a getaway car in a holdup. That night Bob and I drank the whole bottle. I was sick for a day and a half, and I didn't have another drink until I was in college. I still don't like scotch. I don't know whether Mom did that on purpose or whether she just got lucky.

Once I got to college, I had to make up for lost time, and I did. Sometimes I'm surprised that people survive college, especially if they have cars.

Now and then on an afternoon in the middle of the week, when we were bored or exhausted from an entire, uninterrupted hour of studying History or Political Science, somebody would burst into the room and holler a single, magical word: "McSorley's!" After several seconds of argument and deliberation ("Who's driving?"), we would pile into a car and be on our way.

Now, you may be wondering why we began our debauchery so early in the day. Didn't we have work to do? Couldn't we hold off on drinking until after dinner?

Let me remind you that we went to school in Providence, Rhode Island, and McSorley's Old Ale House is in New York City. If we left home in mid-afternoon, we would arrive in Manhattan around dinnertime; and for hors d'oeuvres we would order a plate of saltine crackers and a soft cheese called Liederkranz that was so foul-smelling it isn't even manufactured anymore. The plate also came with large, round, white slices of raw onions, which we would dip in hot mustard before devouring like potato chips. Once, shortly after the saloon began admitting female patrons, a woman seated next to me asked me to breathe in the opposite direction.

McSorley's had waiters (and, after women's liberation, waitresses) with biceps like Charles Atlas. Their hands and fingers were strong, too, and they owed it all to the mugs of ale they carried—in each hand half a dozen, maybe more, and no trays. The drinks always arrived on the table in even numbers. You would buy two or four at a time, and I mean two or four for each person. If you were such a cheapskate and wimp that you tried to split an order, two people taking one glass apiece, you would have a hard time getting the attention of the waiter or bartender again.

My friends outdrank me. I didn't like being a "weak stick," but usually I drank about half as much as my pals. If they drank twenty ales each, I would have ten, maybe twelve. That may sound like a lot, but the mugs at McSorley's were small.

Then we would head home. Ed was the best drunk driver. He could get sloppy drunk, sing-and-fall-down-and-shlur-your-wordsh-drunk; but as soon as he got behind the wheel, he became a different man. It was like when Clark Kent went into a phone booth. Ed got us home without incident many times. Some of our other drivers weren't quite so skillful. I remember standing before a urinal at a rest stop along the New Jersey Turnpike when a group of men came in and started bellowing about some idiot in a Ford Torino who was swerving all over the road. I said nothing.

If you know your geography, you may be wondering why my friends and I, on our way from New York City to Providence, found ourselves in New Jersey. Well, we wondered that, too, sometimes. On those occasions it was just an accident, the result of a navigational error. More often, however, it was deliberate. The bars in New Jersey closed an hour later than the ones in New York, so we made a detour for a nightcap on our way home.

Eat, Drink , and Be

We didn't have to leave our dorm to find the pleasures of alcohol. One night when I was a junior, we had a party that ran late, and I drank to the end. When I woke up the next morning, I was not hung over: I was still drunk. I might have skipped my Shakespeare seminar that morning, except I had to read my term paper to the class. So I went to school and did my duty. Afterwards one of my fellow students praised me. She said that all year long I had been very quiet, hardly saying anything; she thought I was shy. But that morning, reciting my essay, I had been entirely different: hollering, whispering, grabbing people with my eyes, acting out the parts. She said it had been quite a performance.

Liquor will do that sometimes.

Sometimes not.

I don't drink as much as I used to. I rarely exceed two drinks in a sitting when I know I'll have to drive—I would not like to hurt somebody or even to damage my car. Even when I'm safely at home, however, I almost never drink like a college boy anymore. This new-found moderation does not spring from a desire for dignity and decorum but from the same source as my drinking itself— namely, the love of pleasure. A mild inebriation is enjoyable; vomiting or a hangover is not. There is no disgrace, I believe, in planning as far ahead as tomorrow morning. Thus, the relentless pursuit of pleasure enforces the Golden Mean.

So, too, does a concern, however tentative and restricted, for health. The human body, says Tolstoy, is a machine for living; and while that machine is rugged and resilient, to me it seems prudent to spare it a grotesque degree of abuse.

Many years ago, when I went to a doctor's office for a routine physical, he asked a routine question: Do you drink? I said yes. He said, how much? I said, I don't know, maybe four or five a day. The doctor was an evangelical Christian, but he surprised me with his liberality on this issue. Four or five drinks, he said, won't kill you, but there is a tendency for four or five to become six or seven, then eight or ten. He said I should keep an eye on that.

So I did. Ever since that day, I have counted my drinks, recording the score each night before I go to bed, in a pocket calendar I keep in my desk. At the end of each month, I add up the number of drinks, then divide by the number of days. I measure out my life in shot glasses.

At first I thought that my off-the-cuff estimate to the doctor had proved correct. According to my subsequent calculations, I did indeed average four or five drinks a day. But then I remembered the Heisenberg Uncertainty Principle and how the very act of observing an event changes the event itself. I suspected that because I was counting, and because I knew that alcohol could be harmful to me, I was subconsciously holding my consumption *down* to four or five drinks a day. I wondered what it would be if I weren't counting.

Thanks, Doc.

For several years my daily average remained constant. Then, when my bum foot started acting up with arthritis, I went to see a different doctor, a "physiatrist," a specialist in rehabilitation. She said that alcohol was ravaging my nervous system, slowing my reactions, ruining my health. She said the only way I could arrest that decline and perhaps even regain some of my lost reflexes was to drink no more liquor at all. *None!* Of course, she was the same doctor who told me I should reduce stress on my legs by installing a taller toilet. Maybe I'll stop drinking at the same time I remodel the bathroom.

Still, I wonder if my liver is diseased. My blood tests indicate no damage thus far, but I worry about the future. In the last few years I have cut my daily consumption of alcohol from four or five drinks down to three or four. So marginal a reduction would not satisfy my physiatrist, but, for me, it will have to do.

Once, in college, I met a certifiable alcoholic. Actually I've probably met a lot of them, but he was the first I knew was one. He was a gay man who taught at a women's college, but I don't think that's what made him drink. Maybe it was something else about teaching. He told a story about how, one day at the end of a lesson, he asked the class if they had any questions. An eager student raised her hand, and he called on her. "Is it true," she asked, "that you drink a fifth of gin a day?" A sudden silence gripped the classroom, but the professor dispelled it quickly. "Hell!" he replied, "I *spill* that much."

I hope I can conduct myself with as much aplomb as that instructor.

You may be wondering what else I have put in my mouth. If so, naughty you! The truth of the matter is, however, that I have never smoked, not much anyway. Some of my friends in college and grad school used to light up at a bar or a party, and I would bum a cigarette off them. There's a limit to how often you can do that, however: even the best of friends has a limit to his generosity. Therefore, Marlboros and Kools never had much chance to destroy my lungs.

I didn't smoke marijuana until I was in college. There was a party, and *Sergeant Pepper* was on the record player. I had never heard music all around me before. It reminded me of the day I threw out my old record player with its single speaker and replaced it with a two-speakered stereo. I wondered how smoke could make sound come from all directions. I pushed fat handfuls of popcorn into my mouth, and butter coagulated on my chin. Food is good, isn't it? After a while one of my friends took me for a walk around the block, around the block, around the block.

Joints are like regular cigarettes, though: over the years I've smoked quite a few but never actually bought one. My friends are very kind.

Once, in college, we turned our English professor on. She was a woman in her forties or fifties—to the young, all middle-aged people seem the same remote, indeterminate age. In this seminar, however, the discussion turned to marijuana, and the professor mentioned that she had never tried it. One of the bolder students said, "We can fix that." So we had a party at the professor's house. She made chili, and somebody brought weed.

I don't think college classes are like that so much anymore.

There was a younger instructor who taught Intermediate Writing and who was more familiar with recreational drugs than his senior colleague was. I learned a lot from him. He told a story about an older writer who told a younger writer (I don't remember the names, just the words): "You must learn to murder your darlings." I try to remember that quotation whenever I edit my prose. The instructor had above his desk a picture of Queen Victoria at her most daunting. The caption read, in the royal plural: "We are not amused." My teacher told me to remember that warning whenever I tried to write something funny. Not that you shouldn't try, but that you had better succeed.

But the point is that my writing teacher, who taught me when I was a sophomore, died when I was a junior. I later heard that he had thought he was taking LSD, but it turned out to be psilocybin laced with strychnine. The two concoctions have similar effects, up to a point. My teacher went into a coma, struggled for a day or two, then died.

I never tried acid. Not because I had moral objections, nor because I respected or feared the law, nor even (as you may have come to suspect by now) because I was too parsimonious. No, I abstained because I feared the trip itself, the psychic consequences. I didn't worry about dying, not even after my teacher's death, but I worried about going someplace far away and not being able to get back. In short, I was afraid.

Even macrobiotics can be dangerous if you go too far in the direction of either yin or yang. Food is a "substance," a kind of a drug, too, and you can overdose on apples and green tea. What you eat can take your mind to a different place, and isn't that what the Sixties were all about—to boldly go where no man had gone before, except for maybe a billion Indians and Chinese?

And how about fasting? You don't hear much about that nowadays, but it happened. One year, as part of a charitable program at my university, I skipped one meal a week at the refectory. Students who had paid for a meal plan would volunteer to forgo one dinner each week, and for each meal thus sacrificed, the university would donate fifty cents to an agency that fed the poor. Some evenings I entered into the spirit of the event by going hungry— "performing austerities," as we used to call it—and trying to imagine hunger that was neither voluntary nor short-lived. Other evenings, I just went to a restaurant for hot dogs or pizza.

One week in my senior year, however, when I lived off-campus and no longer had a meal plan to forsake, I stopped eating for three consecutive days. This was not an act of charity but an experiment: I wanted to see how my body would react to nutritional deprivation. React it did. I would be watching television, and there would be an advertisement for hamburgers or even canned peas, and I desired them so intensely that I could actually taste them. That was the hungriest I had ever been. In fact, it was practically the only occasion I *had* been hungry for longer than the time it took me to heat a can of soup. I'm afraid that neither fasting nor philosophy has ever freed me from attachment to worldly things.

What was most curious, however, was the psychological effect of starvation. Of course I felt weak and weary. People tell me you get over that if you fast long enough, just as they tell me you get elated if you run for ten miles; but since I never did either, I can't really say. What I can say, however, is that after a couple days without food, I started seeing things: not hallucinations exactly but phenomena I hadn't noticed before, like the lovely multicolored aura that surrounds every blazing light bulb. You don't see that if your belly's full.

After three days, though, I couldn't take the hunger anymore, so I went to an Italian restaurant and ordered chicken cacciatore. This was not wise. Later I learned that when you are ending a fast, you should eat bland foods that are easy on the stomach, like oatmeal. Chicken cacciatore is not like oatmeal. The spices and maybe even the meat itself made my stomach cramp and grind, as if I had been gulping down the bones. On my tongue, though, the dish tasted like something from Paradise, and I survived the pain in my gut.

The only time I fast nowadays is just before a blood test. Food is too important to give up. It gets me through the days.

Chapter Six

❈ The Root of Evil ❈

I f I had ever met my father, I might have asked him
why he had forsaken me. I would not have asked for
money, because I would have known that he had
none.

Mom and Hij—that, you may recall, was my father's
nickname before it became mine—moved into an
apartment house in Spokane, right after getting married in
1946. My father was the building manager. *His* father,
whom my siblings and I always called Grampa, was not the
owner but somehow had invested his life savings in the
property, so I guess that's why Hij got to manage it. Mom
has told me the story of this short-lived enterprise but
doesn't know the details. She says she was too busy
having babies and raising children to pay attention to
business.

Sometimes, though, she couldn't help but notice that
something was going wrong. Tenants would bring their
rent money to Mom, and she would give it to Hij to
deposit at the bank. Instead of doing that, however, he
would take the money and go gambling. Then Mom

would write a check to pay a bill, and the check would bounce. At night sometimes, Mom would be startled from sleep by men banging on the door, demanding the money Hij owed them.

After a while the family had to move out of the apartment house. Grampa had lost all the money he had invested, and he would have to work in coming years at steady but low-paying jobs. In the time I knew him, before he moved to his daughter Sachi's farm in Oregon, he lived in a small apartment where we sometimes stopped on our walk home from church. As for Mom and Hij after their expulsion, they spent a few months at a hotel downtown, then in 1948 moved to a development optimistically named Victory Heights. They were still there when I was born the following year.

Victory Heights was temporary housing built during World War II and torn down in the following decade. I don't remember it at all, but Mom says the building in which we lived looked like the wooden barracks at Tule Lake, the concentration camp in California where her family had spent two years of the war. Unlike in camp, however, each family had its own bathroom. We would not always have that luxury.

Hij got a job as a telegrapher for the SP&S—the Seattle, Portland & Spokane Railroad. It was a good job, but it required him to be away from home for weeks at a time. A few months after my birth he was working in a small town in south-central Washington—Mom doesn't remember which one. He embezzled fifty dollars from the railroad, got caught, got fired, and disappeared. We heard later that he had returned to Portland, the city of his birth. Maybe he was too ashamed to come back to Spokane and face his family, or maybe he just got tired of having a wife and three kids.

Mom thinks he stole the fifty dollars because of his gambling. Maybe he owed money to somebody, the vigorous kind of man who collects his debts without recourse to the legal system. Hij would need cash right away, and the only place he could get it was the company cash register. That's Mom's theory, anyway. She never had a chance to ask.

Japanese like to gamble. When I was in my twenties, I sometimes used to go to the race track in Spokane, and it seemed as if half the nihonjin in town were there. One man my age made a living as a professional gambler, following the horses from track to track in Washington and Oregon. He had to quit that, though, after he got married and had kids and therefore needed a steadier income and domicile. So my father's gambling was very much in keeping with Japanese customs. Deserting his wife and children, however, was not. My family has never been perfectly traditional.

When Mom was dating Hij, she noticed that he seemed to have money even when he didn't have a job. She didn't know about his gambling, though, until their honeymoon, when he took her to the dog track. She says that's the only thing she remembers about her honeymoon.

Hij had been spoiled as a child. Grampa had two boys, but one died in childhood, thus turning Hij into an only son.　After my grandmother died young from tuberculosis, my grandfather doted on my dad.　His older sister Sachiko says that while she had to work at home and in the family grocery store in Portland, her brother never had to do any work at all.　All he did, besides go to school, was play baseball and basketball and edit the sports section of the high school newspaper.　When Hij turned sixteen, he told Grampa he needed a car to get to ballgames.　Grampa bought him a year-old Pontiac, even though all the other kids took a bus to the games.　In those days most Japanese families had no car at all.　So Hij got accustomed to getting everything he wanted without having to work or save.　That's how Mom explains his later problems, anyway.

I've wondered whether the war might have had something to do with it.　Could Hij have suffered from what we would later learn to call post-traumatic stress disorder?　Mom says she doesn't know: he never talked about the war.　He was in some very tough fighting, though, before German shrapnel ended the war for him, just before the Battle of the Bulge.　He earned two Bronze Stars and a Purple Heart.

Aunt Sachi remembers only one story he told her about the war.　He and a buddy, his best friend, were exhausted, so they lay down to rest.　After a while, it was time to move on, so Hij hollered at his pal to get up.　The man didn't move, so Hij rolled him over onto his back. The buddy was dead.

Sachi says that when Hij got back from the war, he was the proverbial "nervous wreck."　He smoked three

A Piece of Valiant Dust

packs of cigarettes a day, and he drank. He had never done that before. Of course, before the war he had been just a high school kid, so maybe he had never had the chance. After getting wounded in France, he was moved from hospital to hospital for treatment, then he went to live with a Japanese family in Portland. The family were gamblers, and Hij used his car to take them to the dog track. Aunt Sach says he never stopped gambling after that.

I always thought my father's experience must have been like what I saw in *Go for Broke!*, the movie about his all-Japanese outfit, the 442nd Regimental Combat Team, starring Van Johnson. The film would be screened at our church every Memorial Day, followed by a trip to the cemetery to lay wreaths and flowers. The scene I remember most vividly is when a wounded G.I., helpless and screaming during an artillery barrage, is crushed by a shell-splintered tree, whose still-vertical trunk descends inexorably upon him like the head of a baseball bat upon an ant. I thought that was what the war was like. Could that turn you into a gambler?

"Go for Broke!" was the motto of the 4-4-2. It was gambling slang meaning "bet it all." The 4-4-2, along with its companion, the all-Japanese 100th Battalion, had more casualties in the war than any other American unit of similar size: ninety-five hundred Purple Hearts in an outfit with only forty-five hundred men when at full strength. Of course, after it got into combat, it was never at full strength. "Go for Broke" is what Hij always did.

128

The Root of Evil

He and Mom got divorced two years after he deserted us. I don't know what the divorce decree stipulated, but Mom never received child support, much less alimony. A few years after the divorce, Hij wanted to get back together with Mom, but she said no. Later he married a white woman in Portland but didn't have any more kids.

One year Hij gave us Christmas presents. Bob and I got battery-powered toy cars with remote control, and Jan got a stuffed animal, a dog with floppy ears. All the other years, though, there was nothing. Long afterward, Aunt Sachi explained that one year of bounty. She had told her brother that he ought to visit his children, so he bought presents and went to Spokane. When he got there, though, Mom asked if he had brought us any *money*. He said no, so she would not let him see us kids. He left the presents with her.

Later somebody took a photograph of Jan holding the toy dog and smiling broadly, rejoicing in the generosity of her father. Mom sent the photo to her brother, my Uncle Hank. On the back, my mother wrote, "This makes me sick."

When I was in graduate school, I got word that my father was dying of Hodgkin's Disease. Mom asked if I wanted to visit him, but I said no. I didn't know the man and didn't want to start now. After I heard that he had died, I wrote "father, father, father" in a notebook and observed that to me the word was unfamiliar. What *is* a father anyway? He was forty-nine or fifty when he died, but I don't know which, because I don't know his birthday. His estate consisted of an automobile;

apparently his gambling had prevented him from accumulating any other property. Each of his children was entitled to a share of the car, but we waived our claims, so his wife could have it. She deserved something.

After Hij deserted us, our family became transients, living briefly in different places. We didn't own any trunks or suitcases; so each time we moved, Mom would pack our clothes in shopping bags. There wasn't much to pack. We lived a few months with my Uncle Bob, then a year with my Auntie Toko and Uncle Fred.

Fred and Toko were childless. In those days, nobody asked why. For me, however, the important fact is that they offered to relieve my mother's poverty by adopting me.

The proposal made a lot of sense. Toko and Fred would finally have a child; and for Japanese as old-fashioned as they were, it might have been especially gratifying to have a *son*. Mom would still have Bob and Jan, and all she would have to give up was her second, superfluous boy. The logic for an exchange was incontrovertible. Nevertheless, my mother resisted.

Then Ma-chan, Uncle Fred's sister, joined the discussion. Ma-chan said it was wrong to break up a family, separating the children. Mom felt relieved to have someone else in the family firmly make this point. Mom thanked Fred and Toko for their offer but said no. Had she not done so, my last name today would be Yamamoto.

We could have stayed longer with Fred and Toko, but my aunt had definite ideas about the proper rearing of children, and my mother did not share them. Once, for example, Mom told us kids we could play with some pots and pans; these were what we used in lieu of ordinary toys. My aunt, however, said no: it was *her* house, so we would abide by *her* rules. In 1952 we moved out of that house and into a red brick apartment house downtown. It was called the Insley and was the first place I remember occupying, the scene of my first memories.

We had two rooms: a kitchenette and a bedroom—no living room. The bathroom was a communal one at the end of a long hall. One of my first memories is walking down that hall toward the bathroom but glancing to the left, through an open door, and seeing a ghost flutter through a darkened room. Maybe it was just a white shirt or towel dangling on a clothesline, but I ran back to our apartment in terror. Another memory is of taking a bath in the kitchen. When any of us kids had measles or chickenpox, Mom would not want to expose other people to our germs by using the communal bathtub, so she bought a large, round, chrome-colored tub in which to bathe us. It was fun to take a bath on the floor of the kitchen.

A vacant lot lay next to the Insley, and in the dirt there we planted carrot seeds from a packet Bob and Jan had swiped from a rack in a store. (Apparently I was too young to be included in larceny.) The carrots never came up, which probably disappointed my brother and sister more than me, who always hated carrots. Jan thinks we may have moved to a different neighborhood before the carrots had time to grow, but I suspect they never had a chance in that stony soil.

At our new home, a two-story frame house at the corner of Fifth and Oak, we had a real garden. Actually the garden occupied the corner, and our house faced Oak Street, with a dirt driveway and a detached garage lying between the garden and the house. Since we had no car, we asked Mom if we could keep a horse in the garage, but she said no.

When we first moved in, we lived in the apartment upstairs: kitchen, living room, one bedroom, and full bath. The only phone—shared with the tenants downstairs— was in the hallway on the first floor, so it was a nuisance to have to run downstairs to answer it. A year later we moved to the downstairs apartment, which had *two* bedrooms but a bathroom with nothing but a toilet and a sink—not really a *bath*room at all. To bathe we had to go upstairs to the lavatory we shared with a young married couple who lived above us.

Before long the young couple moved out, and we took over the whole house. Each of us had a private bedroom—mine was what used to be the living room upstairs. Our landlord did not make us pay additional rent when we expanded our living quarters. I think he was kind to us because we were Japanese like him or maybe just because he was kind. He was rich for a Japanese, owning a grocery next to the apartment house where Grampa lived.

I suppose that if an outsider looked at our house, he would find signs of low rent: peeled paint, broken boards, shabby furnishings. I don't deny that these deficiencies existed; it's just that if they did, I never noticed them.

I did notice the pill bugs—elongated gray ovals whose shells were segmented like the tails of their larger fellow crustaceans, the lobsters—that crawled over the damp walls of our basement. If you flipped a bug over, it would curl into a perfect ball that, with the flick of a finger, you could send skittering across the cold cement floor. Then there was the occasional soft mouse we trapped with cheese or peanut butter, and killed, and sorrowfully threw in the trash.

Most of all, however, I noticed the cockroaches. If you came into the kitchen for a glass of water in the middle of the night, you would find them scuttling over the sink, the stove, the walls, the table where we ate. They were small roaches, smaller than the two-inch monsters that I, as a child, observed in the dark basement of an old hotel downtown, but still it was unpleasant to share a house with them. There was something annoying about their crisp, bright brown shells, their thrusting feelers, their tiny, scurrying legs. People said they smelled bad when squashed, but I never noticed that as I swatted them with a rolled-up newspaper or sometimes even with my fingertips. Many years later, when I studied German in college, the scholars would argue over what kind of bug Gregor Samsa turned into; but I knew it was a cockroach because that was the *Ungeziefer* that I loathed most.

One day we decided to get rid of the roaches. We went to a gas station and bought a spray can of insecticide called Shell Tox that was said to be deadlier than anything we could get in the supermarket. We waited until evening, after supper, then observed the creatures' little antennae, pair by pair, jutting up from the crack between a strip of molding and the wall above the kitchen sink. Mom pressed the button on top of the can and sprayed in a long swoosh all down the line.

Suddenly the air was filled with cockroaches, a volcano of vermin, an insectiferous Fourth of July! Roaches soared, veered, tumbled through space. Who knew they could fly? Who knew their hard brown backs were actually wings? Who knew that in the excitement of dying they could crowd the air like locusts or bees? After a moment of astonishment and revulsion, we swatted at them, slapped them out of our hair and off our shoulders. Jan fled the room but still remembers how they dropped from the ceiling; Bob and I enjoyed the combat. The poisoned bugs fell on tables and countertops, fell on the floor, but still lived. They lay on their backs, their legs furiously churning. Soon, though, their exertions would slow, becoming stiffly mechanical, as if the creatures were just going through the motions of resisting fate. Then the legs would stop altogether, bent and rigid in the air. Mom continued spraying, around the wastebasket, under the sink, sometimes pausing to give a second blast to the wounded. We boys crushed them with our hands or under the balls of our gyrating feet.

This event made a lasting impression on my young mind. Forty years later, after being severely disappointed by the facilities and service at a hotel in midtown Manhattan, I relieved my frustration by lying on my back on the bed, wearing nothing but my T-shirt and undershorts, and thrashing my arms and legs through the air. "What are you doing?" my wife inquired. "The Dying Cockroach," I replied.

The great roach massacre was only a partial success, however. Although their number was diminished, the beasts proved resilient and quickly restored their multitude. Spraying Shell Tox became a routine. We could not afford a professional exterminator, so we had to accept cockroaches as a fact of life. When we finally moved out of the Oak Street house, we carefully inspected our boxes and furniture to make sure we did not take a colony of vermin with us.

We never had a car when I was young. When we moved to a new house, it was always within walking distance of school. Of course, walking distance in those days was longer than today. If, however, we had to go clear across town for some reason, we would take a bus or hitch a ride with a neighbor. I disliked depending on neighbors, though, because they did not always share my devotion to punctuality. I hated being late for band practice or even church, time after time, and not being able to do anything about it. When somebody is kind enough to give you a ride, you cannot reproach him for tardiness.

Uncle Fred often gave us rides in his Mercury, then later his big green Buick, and he was always on time. When I was in high school, he helped teach me to drive, then lent me his car whenever I had a date. Those borrowings were complicated, however, since he and

Auntie Toko lived on the other side of town from me. He would drive to my house, then I would drive him home before picking up the girl. After the date, I would drive back to Fred's house, and he would drive me home, then he would have to drive himself home. These dates were my introduction to the science of logistics. As luck would have it, however, I didn't have many of them to worry about.

Providing transportation was not the only way that Fred and Toko helped my family. They took us on week-long vacations of swimming and fishing at a lake. Uncle Fred gave Bob and me an ancient baseball glove with five flat fingers and no pocket, so it looked like an actual hand instead of a leather bowl. It might have been worth something today as a collector's item if we hadn't thrown it away as soon as we got mitts that would actually hold the ball.

Fred and Toko's house was the usual setting for Japanese holiday feasts. We gathered at their table in the dining room, presided over by a mahogany statue of the Buddha, to whom we made offerings of oranges and rice. Uncle Fred played Japanese music on the record player, and I looked through colorful picture magazines that opened from the back and were written in a script I did not understand. Fred and Toko gave us presents for Christmas and birthdays, and sometimes Toko would even pay us a dollar for a picture we drew with crayons.

My uncle and aunt were rich only in comparison to us. Fred was a laborer on the Great Northern Railroad, laying and repairing track. He was a hard worker, skilled and dependable, but could never become a foreman because his English was poor. Toko worked for several years as a waitress at a Skid Row restaurant called the Quality Cafe.

Uncle Hank, brother to Mom and Toko, was a bachelor, so he could serve as our Rich Uncle. Because he moved to Portland, then San Francisco, where he worked in the mysterious new field of computer programming, he could not help us on an everyday basis like Fred and Toko; but he sent us presents regularly and brought more whenever he visited. He gave us the money for the train trips we took to San Francisco and even Los Angeles. How else could we get to Disneyland?

We also depended on the kindness of strangers. After my father left, we went on Aid to Dependent Children (ADC), and we stayed on it until all three of us kids were in school. Nowadays Welfare mothers have to get a job and send their kids to day care as soon as the youngest child is two or even one; but when I was young, the country had family values. Even after Mom went to business school and got a job as a bookkeeper for an insurance company, ADC paid a neighbor to mind us children between the time we came home from school and the time Mom came home from work. That arrangement lasted just a year or two, until we were old enough to take care of ourselves.

We got lots of things for free. Schooling, of course— private schools were unthinkable until I got a scholarship to college—but also the public library. At first Mom walked us there, but soon we went on our own. For me independence was necessary because in the summer I went to the library several times a week: six books was the most they would let me borrow at once. Of course those books were short and easy—I read practically everything by Thornton Burgess—but still I spent much of my childhood in a world created by words.

The Boy Scouts were free, and so was the school band. Then there were occasional acts of individual generosity. In high school I wanted to attend a two-week summer institute at a university in Oregon—sort of a practice run for college. I couldn't afford the tuition, but the Chamber of Commerce arranged to have it paid by a kind businessman.

Some people believe in the self-made man, and my brother the conservative rails against "Welfare bums." I know, however, that my family could not have survived without receiving plenteous gifts from all and sundry.

Not that all we ever did was collect ADC. My mother worked for one insurance company, then another, then got a job with the state in, of all places, the Department of Public Assistance. She worked first as a file clerk, then as a dictating machine transcriber. When she found that the blaring dictaphone had damaged her hearing, she became a receptionist. Then she got promoted to eligibility examiner.

For this last role, however, she was unsuited. She often found that applicants desperately needed help but did not meet all the legal requirements, so she felt anguish when she had to turn them down and advise them to apply to a private charity. Sometimes the rejected applicant would get furious at her, as if the denial were her fault.

Sometimes the Welfare Rights Organization sponsored appeals of her decisions; and although she never had to go through a protracted legal process, she feared having to do so.

All this created anxieties Mom did not need. She asked to be demoted from eligibility examiner back down to clerk, which created a crisis in her office because nobody had ever requested a demotion before, so no one knew how to do the necessary paperwork. Eventually, though, Mom got her wish. Nobody in my family has ever striven for the highest possible income. A living wage and an early retirement—that's all we ask.

Bob and I got paper routes as soon as we could, which in those days was at the age of twelve. Back then a paperboy was an entrepreneur, responsible not only for delivering the papers but also for collecting the payments from subscribers and using that money to reimburse the company for the papers he had received. A couple nights a week I would go door to door, rapping seven times in quick succession, then hollering through the closed door, "Collect, *Review*!" (The *Spokesman-Review* was the morning paper; in our younger years Bob and I had had routes for the evening *Chronicle*, which didn't have a Sunday edition and therefore didn't pay as much.) Most customers paid a month in advance, but some would not. One old woman insisted on paying for only one week at a time, so I would have to go to her back door every week and listen to her complain about what poor service I provided and how worthless the paper was anyway. Many customers were hard to find at home, so they would fall weeks or even months behind in payment. Then, sometimes, they would skip town. If a customer gypped you out of, say, a dollar and a half, that would mean that you had delivered your papers one day for nothing.

I would get up each morning at 3:45, so by 4:00 I could be at the corner where my bundle of papers was dropped from a truck. I snipped the wire that wrapped them, then loaded them into my white canvas bag: a single bag I wore on my left side, with a strap over my right shoulder, when the papers were light; or a double bag with pouches in front and back and a hole for my head in between, like a sarape, when the papers were heavy, as on a Thursday or especially a Sunday. I would have between seventy (weekday) and a hundred thirty (Sunday) papers to deliver. I could usually finish in an hour or less on every day but Sunday. On Sunday I would sometimes pay my sister fifty cents to help me. After finishing my route on weekdays, I would go back to bed for an hour before getting up for school.

I made extra money when it snowed during the night. I had an arrangement with several of my customers that as soon as I finished my route, I would come back and shovel their sidewalks and driveways. By the time they woke up in the morning, their snow would be gone. I wish I could pay a kid to do that for me now.

Thanks to our paper routes, Bob and I always had money, but we spent it as fast as we got it. When I had an afternoon route, I would begin and end my delivery by buying bottles of root beer or orange pop at the gas station, thus squandering a large fraction of the money I

would make that day.   Bob and I used to treat the family
to gallons of root beer, half-gallons of ice cream, and large
bags of potato chips, Corn Nuts, and Fritos. Sometimes
we would go to a hamburger joint and come home with a
bag full. My mother used to ask me if I had a hole in my
pocket. I would say no, why do you ask? She would say,
well, then, what happened to all your money?

My mother, though, was no model of tight-fistedness.
We lived a block from the railroad tracks (our
neighborhood was so poor that both sides of the tracks
were the wrong side), and hoboes would come to our
house to ask for food. I suspect they left a mark in front
of our house to inform their brethren—hoboes had a
written code of their own—because they always knew to
go around to the back door and knock. Mom told us not
to answer the door if we were alone. When she was home,
however, she would ask the man to wait on the porch
while she made a sandwich for him. They kept coming.

In the summer before I started eighth grade, we left
Oak Street and moved a few blocks up the South Hill,
though not as far as where the streets become luxuriously
curvaceous instead of straight.   We had to move because
Interstate 90 was coming through: the spot where our old
house once stood is now part of a strip of urban desert,
livened by milkweed and bachelor buttons, bordering six
broad lanes of federally funded asphalt.

I got rich during my junior year of high school.
Having obtained a job as a copyboy for the *Spokesman-
Review*, I quit my paper route and moved upstairs from

Circulation to Editorial. The pay was only minimum wage, but I worked thirty-five hours a week, so I made a lot of money for a teen-ager. For the first time in my life I saved a substantial sum. Not for college, though. For a car!

Until I bought mine, our family had never had one. It was a three-year-old, brown, four-on-the-floor, unsafe-at-any-speed 1963 Chevy Corvair. Of course I loved it. So *what* if I had to leave the windows cracked open, even in winter, to release the gas fumes that always built up inside! I liked the sound of the wind whistling through the windows anyway, the sound of speed.

The car gave me freedom and a sense of dignity. I did not have to get rides from other people anymore; I could give *them* rides. I worked on the high school newspaper as well as the metropolitan one; and when it was time for the bi-weekly trip to the school's print shop, I felt like a prince taking other students in my car.

I taught my mother and sister how to drive. I remember being in the passenger seat, watching Mom, her arms and hands taut with anxiety, her stiff torso leaning forward, her face so close to the windshield that her fast, heavy breathing would fog it on a cold day. Once, she was making a left turn, and I advised her not to turn too sharply. She maneuvered the car at an angle of forty-five degrees, then came to a stop just before thumping into the curb on the opposite corner. "But," I amended my instruction, "do *turn*." My sister, riding in the back seat as a fellow learner, laughed out loud. Mom practically cried with frustration and humiliation, and I felt remorse for the rest of the day. There are some jokes that should not be told.

Mom did learn to drive—not an easy thing when you're over forty and the car has a standard transmission. Jan learned, too. When I went off to college, I left my car at home, so Mom inherited it.

I went to college with scholarships and loans that paid for my tuition, room, and board. To cover other expenses, like a trip home once or twice a year, I worked one year in the school cafeteria, then one at a Boys' Club. After that, the university increased my scholarship enough so I didn't need any outside job at all. Of course, I had to work every summer, and that usually provided enough savings to carry me through the school year.

For my first three years of college I lived on campus. As a senior, however, I shared an apartment with two friends. Our income was low enough that we qualified for food stamps, but I refused my share. I had already received enough Welfare for one lifetime, and I figured I could get along without more. However, I had no such scruples about taking gifts from my buddies. I often stayed at their homes during vacations, and I always accepted rides in their cars, whether it was to Florida for spring break or just to an after-hours bar on a Saturday night, or even a Thursday.

My own car was back in Spokane, but not for long.

One day my sister, Jan, was driving it; and her fiancé, Jim, was in the passenger seat. Mom was in back. They came to an intersection, and a drunk coming toward them took a left turn and smashed into them head-on. Jan and

Jim were unhurt; they had their seatbelts on. The back seat of the Corvair, however, was not equipped with belts. Mom hurtled forward, and her right knee crashed into the doorhandle, breaking bones.

Jim wrote to tell me what had happened. It was the first letter he had ever sent me, so as soon as I saw the handwriting on the envelope, I had a premonition that something was up. Jim said that Mom had been wearing a wig on the day of the accident. At the moment of impact, the wig flew forward from the back seat and came to rest on the dashboard in front of Jim, looking like roadkill. I thought the event must have been like a scene from a movie, maybe the Three Stooges. I almost laughed.

Mom spent a few weeks in the hospital and many months recuperating at home. She got a metal plate installed in her knee that would sometimes set off the alarm at airport security, until she had the plate removed. For years after that, she got along fine, without even a limp. The surgeon told her, however, that she probably would get arthritis in her knee eventually; and, sure enough, the aches began a few years ago. It grew so severe that she had to have her knee replaced.

In the crash that injured Mom, my car was totally destroyed. The driver who hurt my mother was convicted on several counts. When an ambulance had arrived to pick up Mom, the drunk had tried to elude justice by driving away. In so doing, he had plowed into the ambulance. He wasn't hard to convict.

Mom sued him for damages, pain, and suffering. After Mom's lawyer took his share of the settlement, Mom wound up with three thousand dollars. By the time she got it, I was finishing college and about to start graduate school. I had a fellowship that paid my tuition, but I needed money for the first year's room and board. Mom's three thousand dollars just covered it. I have always said that my professional education was bought with my mother's blood.

Financially, graduate school was like college all over again. I had gotten scholarships to pay my college tuition; and in my second year of grad school, I got a teaching assistantship that paid for all my expenses. I kept getting TA's until my sixth year, as I was finishing my dissertation, when I got a temporary but full-time instructorship at a college across town. I take satisfaction, if not pride, in never having paid a penny for tuition at any level of schooling.

My salary as an instructor enabled me to leave a house shared by four other grad students and to get an apartment of my own. It was in an old, subdivided house owned by a man who had quit his job as a professor of political science in order to become a roofer because of the longer vacations: he said he now worked six months, then collected unemployment for the next six. I'll bet he also made large profits off his rental properties, however, because he didn't spend much on their upkeep. My apartment had something that brought back memories of childhood: cockroaches. I complained to the landlord, who blamed them on unfastidious housekeeping by the woman in the apartment below mine. Late one night, or actually early in the morning, as I typed a lecture I was to deliver in a few hours, I glanced down at the bourbon and soda on my desk. A roach had managed to get inside the glass and was straddling a white ice cube: a six-legged Peary or Amundsen. If nuclear winter, an era of ice induced by atomic fire, ever freezes all humankind to death, cockroaches will inherit the Earth. You have to admire their endurance.

As a grad student, I didn't have a car, but who needed one in a city as small as Ithaca, New York? My legs took me up and down the hills, and in a pinch I could take a bus or cadge a ride with a friend. In my second year of full-time teaching—now certified as a Ph.D. and promoted to assistant professor—I bought my second car, a used Volkswagen Beetle. I wanted to make sure it was sound, so I paid a mechanic fifty dollars to check it out. He said it was fine, so I bought it. A year later I was driving through Hartford, Connecticut, when the brakes went out suddenly and completely, and I coasted through a red light to an eventual stop in front of a shopping mall. My car, I found, was rusted through and through, a total loss. Since that time I have not trusted used cars, used-car dealers, or auto mechanics—at least not in Ithaca, New York.

After my Volkswagen died, I bought a Honda Civic hatchback that I called a hearse for midgets even though it was white. It was brand-new but economical: no frivolous doodads like automatic transmission or air conditioning. By the time I got it, I was an assistant professor, on a tenure track, at a small public university in Massachusetts. The pay was modest, and it didn't rise much because the government went several years without appropriating funds for raises. Still, I was richer than ever before.

I wouldn't be poor again until I spent a sabbatical doing research at Berkeley. That year I received only half my normal salary, so I couldn't afford an apartment. I rented a room in a house in Oakland. I shared a kitchen with the landlady and another tenant, and I was allotted one shelf in the communal refrigerator. Half my space was filled with beer.

It was a very good year.

Chapter Seven

❄ The Game Game ❄

Play makes everybody a god or at least an aspiring novelist. It incites the imagination, turning a driveway into a baseball park, or a living room carpet into a battlefield. Play enables anybody to create a world.

A game is a structured form of play. Sometimes I think life is nothing but a game, but that's only when I'm euphoric. Games are fair: they have rules that are the same for everyone. Experience and statistics create a calming predictability, but one of the things you can predict is surprise. Most important, games give you a chance, many chances, to do something right, even when your work and your world are venues of perpetual failure. You should never go an entire day without succeeding at *something*.

My mother has always liked to play. Of all the moms in the neighborhood, mine was the only one who played in the street with the kids. It's not that she had more time than the other mothers: she had a full-time job as well as a house to keep up and three children to superintend. I guess it's just that she liked to play with us. She played

softball on the street in front of our house, and she walked
down the block to the schoolground with us to shoot
baskets. On the lawn by the driveway she stood with feet
apart and knees bent as she whirled a hula hoop above her
hips—more successfully than I.

Not that she was an athlete. She wasn't particularly
muscular, fleet, or adroit; not notably proficient at hitting a
softball or sinking hoops. She had not engaged in
organized sports since playing guard in a Japanese girls'
basketball league in high school. She certainly wasn't big:
five feet one or two in those days, though now she's
shrunk to somewhere in the fours—the *high* fours, she
would insist. No, she didn't play because she had unusual
talent to exploit or even because she wanted to teach
athletic skills to her children. She did it because she
wanted to play with us. Let's break that down: (1) to
play—to join the game; (2) with us—to be with her
children.

We played softball in two leagues: the Street League
and the Driveway League. I remember Mom only in the
Street League. Maybe that's because that league required
more players: a pitcher, a catcher, a first baseman, a fielder
or two, and a couple batters. When Mom and some
neighbor kids joined us, we could play on Oak Street.

Mostly, though, we performed in the Driveway
League. Home plate was an unmarked spot in the dirt in
front of our garage, whose permanently closed door (we
had no car) did the job of a catcher. First base was the tall,
splintering, wooden fencepost at one corner of the garden.
It was only six feet from the pitcher's "mound," which

actually wasn't raised at all, so the pitcher did double-duty as first baseman. Second base was the rusty green pole holding a yellow sign—"SCHOOL ZONE"—across the street from the pitcher. Third base was the stump of a tree, sliced down even with the lawn, back on our side of the street and fifteen feet to the right of the pitcher, who could cover that base as well. We only needed one or two fielders and a hitter or two. However, a runner had to look both ways before dashing from first to second or from second to third. Sometimes we would have to stop the game to let a car go by. We muttered, "What do you think this is, *a street?* "; but we never got up the nerve to yell that at the driver. After all, anybody driving through our neighborhood probably lived there.

My brother Bob and I often played by ourselves, with one of us as the entire team in the field and the other as the entire lineup. If you hit a ground ball past the pitcher, it was a single. If the ball reached the street on the fly, it was a double. Across the street, a triple. If the ball cleared the sidewalk across the street, home run! If there were men on base, they would be imaginary ones who would advance as many bases as the man at bat.

On rare occasions somebody clobbered the ball to right-center field, sending it streaking through the branches of a tall spruce tree and into the side of a neighbor's house. Usually it bounced harmlessly off the clapboards, but once it smashed a window. Our own house was closer to the plate and even more vulnerable, though it was in foul territory on the third base side. We broke a living room window or two, and once the window right above the pillows on Mom's bed exploded. I guess she wasn't in bed at the time, because she has only a dim recollection of the event.

You may ask—Mom might have asked—why we, when intent on playing softball, did not walk the one block down to the schoolyard. Well, it was a long block, and it's more fun playing at home. Besides, the diamond at school was regulation size for softball, with a large infield and outfield, which meant we would need more players than we had. No, the driveway was the best place to play.

Bob was the only member of the family to demonstrate any athletic ability. My sister Jan and I never learned to ride a bike, but Bob did. In baseball he learned to switch-hit. He played Little League in the summer, and he tried out for the high school freshman team but didn't make it. That was no disgrace, though, because his class had eight hundred students. When we moved later to Monroe Street, Bob played ping-pong with the firemen in the station across the street, and he learned to put such spin on the ball that I had no chance against him unless he spotted me to at least a ten-point handicap. We set up our table in the wide archway between the dining room and the living room.

Janice played softball as a kid, but it wasn't possible for a girl to play sports after that, at least not in our neighborhood, where middle-class pastimes like golf and tennis were as inconceivable as polo. Jan wasn't muscular, so Bob and I used to have an endurance contest in which we would take turns allowing her to sock us in the stomach, a little harder each time, until she was hitting as hard as she could. She probably would have slugged harder if she wasn't laughing so much. After she got married and moved to southern California, she became a good tennis player. Bob and I wouldn't let her punch us in the stomach after that. Jan is the only one of us siblings who today might be described as "slim."

I'm less athletic than either Bob or Jan. I never even played actual baseball. Irving School had a playground made of asphalt, not grass or dirt, so we couldn't play hardball there. Even softball was difficult, especially when you slid into a base. I played softball through eighth grade, on a team so bad that we had to let seventh graders join us as ringers. We lost to Whittier School, which had fewer students than Irving, and we got slaughtered by Lincoln. You know who goes to a school named Lincoln.

My career in basketball was even less successful. I played only one year—sixth grade, as I recall. Our team must have had more than five players, because I spent almost the whole season on the bench. Finally, though, in a game in which our opponents had an insurmountable lead—ten points, maybe—Coach put me in. I enjoyed a few minutes of genial futility, as a mobile spectator, hauling myself from one end of the court to the other but being careful not to get too close to either basket, which is where you could get hurt.

Despite my avoidance of contention, however, I collided with somebody, or maybe one of my feet took issue with the other. I ended up seated on the floor near the foul line, with my legs apart and my head in a daze. I looked up, far away, and saw the other boys battling for the ball. Somebody slapped it high into the air; and I saw it arcing, slowly and softly, toward me, until it landed in my lap. I held it in front of my face, wondering what to do with the thing. I saw several large boys, total strangers, running toward me, their faces suggesting malign intent. In a kind of rational panic, I threw the ball up, in the general direction of the basket. In a kind of miracle, it went in. Thus I scored the only two points of my entire interscholastic basketball career.

Besides softball, there were other games we played outside when we were small. With the neighborhood kids and Bob and Jan, I played the games common in those times: hide and seek, kick the can, tag. I disliked all those games, though, because success depended on running, and I was always the slowest kid around. Mother, May I? required more thought than speed, but that was a girls' game.

No, my preference was for sedentary indoor games. Bob and I invented several of them. One, a variant of marbles, we called Santa Anna, after the Mexican general whose troops killed Davy Crockett on TV. With chalk we would draw parallel lines, perhaps six feet apart, all the way across the frayed, napless gray carpet of the living room. Bob would line up his marbles on one line, and mine would man the other. One of us would be the Americans and the other the Mexicans, though to the unpracticed eye the two armies looked exactly alike. Then, using our favorite shooters, we would take turns sniping at the opposite side, knocking them off the wall of the Alamo

(Americans) or dead in their trench (Mexicans). Bob shot in the "knuckles" fashion, but I never got the hang of that, so always shot "thumbsies." Sometimes we played just for fun, but it was *more* fun to play for keeps. How else can you understand—really understand, with either elation or numb despair—what people mean when they say that somebody "won all the marbles"? You can't comprehend the metaphorical unless you have experienced the actual.

Our favorite game, though, was Baseball Cards. We had thousands of cards, and we invented a way to play with them. Each of us would choose a twenty-five-man team, sometimes consisting of an actual team like the Yankees or the Dodgers, sometimes an All-Star Team from the American or National League. We would get out two or more decks of playing cards, removing the jokers but using four of them face-down as the bases. Then we would shuffle the rest of the cards and flip them over one by one.

The pitcher would go first, then the batter. If the pitcher's card was higher, the pitch was a strike; if the same as the batter's, a foul ball. In our league there were lots of strikeouts. If the batter's card was one to four numbers higher than the pitcher's, the pitch was called a ball. But if the batter beat the pitcher by five or more, the ball was in play. Then the pitcher and batter would each turn over another card. If the pitcher won, the batter was out. If the two tied, the batter was still out, but only because of a spectacular catch dramatically announced, as if on radio, by whoever's team was in the field.

The Game Game

If the batter won by one to four numbers, he had a single; five or six, a double; seven, a triple—these were appropriately rare; eight or more, a home run. Our league had plenty of homers, and the pitcher knew he was in trouble if he turned over a two. We had base stealing, too. If there was a man on base, the batter could yell "There he goes!" before the pitcher turned over his next card. If that card beat the batter's next one, the runner was out; a tie went to the runner. Stealing home was not at all unusual.

You can play this game if you like. Bob and I never applied for a copyright.

We spent thousands of hours looking at baseball cards, mostly studying the rough gray backs with all the statistics. For some years in the late 1950s and early 1960s I knew not only the previous year's numbers for many players but also their career numbers, at least for the important categories like wins, earned run average, strikeouts, batting average, home runs, runs batted in, put-outs, assists, errors, and fielding percentage. In those days cards used to include defensive statistics, which is no longer true in these steroidal, home-run-worshiping times.

My favorite card was of a catcher for the Baltimore Orioles named Frank Zupo. When I arranged my cards alphabetically, he was near the end, behind Norm Zauchin, Gus Zernial, and Don Zimmer, and ahead of only George Zuverink. On Zupo's first and last card, in 1958, he had bushy black eyebrows that converged, chest hair that straggled up to his throat, and a batting average of .083. His name, face, and average have stuck in my mind ever since. Sometimes I would put Frank Zupo on a team with

Mickey Mantle and Ted Williams, and he would hit just as well as they did.

Bob and I gambled for baseball cards, as well as just about everything else (comic books, toys, and of course money). Usually we played poker. I was more prudent than Bob, so often I would end up winning all his worldly possessions. Sometimes, though, he would refuse to pay up. When I complained to Mom, she would tell me I shouldn't gamble with a welsher.

We also gambled with a blond boy named Hal. His father owned a motel, so Hal had enough money to go to the grocery store and fill a paper bag with packs of baseball cards. Then he would play poker with Bob and me and lose them all. He lost consistently because my brother and I had devised a highly successful method of cheating. I don't recall what it was, but I believe it involved signaling. One day Hal accused Bob and me of not playing fairly. When we denied it, he proclaimed, "You lie. You *lie!*" There was something in his tone of voice—high-pitched indignation combined with an amazement that bordered on delight—that I can never forget. He seemed to revel in his discovery of others' corruption. To ourselves, Bob and I justified our dishonesty by reasoning that a rich kid could afford to lose his baseball cards. I guess we were right, because Hal kept coming back.

My most vivid memory of Hal, however, concerns a softball game. It was in the driveway, he was pitching, and I stood in the batter's box in front of the garage. Hal had to blow his nose but did not resort to a handkerchief. Instead he pressed one forefinger against a nostril and, with a flick of his head perfectly coinciding with a blast of air from his sinuses, flung a rope of mucus that ended up clinging to the wooden fencepost that served as first base. Obviously he had practiced this move, and I had to admire it. I was a little careful, however, the next time I slapped my hand on first as I ran past, minding more than the usual splinters.

My family played many table games. Besides a Japanese card game called *hana*, we engaged in the usual American ones: pinochle (three- or four-handed; single-deck or double-), rummy, Monopoly, Life, Tripoley, Pit, Racko, Risk, and Milles Bornes. I won't even mention the faddish games we played only a few times. Bob and I spent many hours prone on the living room carpet playing two-man games like chess, checkers, Chinese checkers, war (high man wins), Stratego, Battleship, and 1863. Was it a sign of the times (after World War II and Korea but before Vietnam) that there were so many military games, or was that just because we were boys?

We also played word games. Scrabble, Anagrams, Probe—these were some of our favorites. My Aunt Peggy, Uncle Bob's wife, was unbeatable at Dig, a game in which you frantically rummaged through a pile of cardboard squares containing letters of the alphabet, seeking the right ones to form a word. It was important to choose an easy word. When the game suddenly called for, say, the name of a river, Peggy would dive through the stack to a P and an O while I would be lost looking for something like C, O, L, U, M, B, I, A.

Then there was Hangman, in which one player, the hangman, would choose a word and the other player, the condemned man, would desperately try to guess it. Using paper and pencil, the hangman would sketch a gallows and, underneath, a series of dashes—one for each letter of the secret word. The prisoner would guess a letter; and if it were in the word, the hangman would write the letter above the appropriate dash. But if it were not, the hangman would draw one body part of a stick figure standing on the gallows: a circle for the head, then straight lines for the torso, arms, and legs. If the condemned did not evade his doom by discovering the secret word, then finally would appear the rope and the noose, which would cinch his windpipe and snap his neck. Amidst the cheerful violence of children's imagination, it paid to know words.

My cousin Dave used to enjoy coming to our house because we were always playing games. I guess his family didn't do that. Maybe most families don't.

Games were not the only form of play, and I didn't always need people to play with. Solitude is the soil in which imagination grows, and solitude was one natural resource of which I have always possessed an abundance.

I also had toy soldiers. I would set them up and knock them down, set them up and knock them down, but a little differently each time, with each death a different story. My favorite set of soldiers consisted of GIs from World War II, all made of hard, green rubber. There was a man kneeling behind a machine gun, a marksman lying prone behind a Browning Automatic Rifle, a soldier standing with feet apart and one arm stretched back, his hand clutching a grenade. These were all Americans, though. I didn't have any Germans or Japanese, so there was nobody for my army to fight. Sometimes I would get out a model airplane and use it to mow down my troops. Most often, though, they were massacred by some unseen and immaterial force: Death itself.

I had a set of Revolutionary War soldiers, with both Americans (blue) and British (red, obviously). However, in a fit of patriotic fervor, I gave half the Redcoats to a friend of mine, since I considered them undesirable. This left the remaining British badly outnumbered, however, and I didn't feel good about letting the Patriots win a contest so unfair. Toy soldiers ought to be sporting.

I also had a set of medieval knights, whose armor was a dull gray rather than "shining." They defended a castle with battlemented walls, a tower with a peaked roof topped by a waving yellow pennon, and a drawbridge that could be raised and lowered. Sometimes I would stage a "Battle Royal," in which all my soldiers, from whatever era, would fight. A knight on horseback, his lance pointed low, would charge out of the castle and onto the drawbridge, only to be instantly disarticulated by a GI's bazooka.

The World War II and Revolution soldiers were the best ones in terms of manufacturing: sturdy, pliable, three-dimensional figurines. However, I also had troops made of brittle, flat plastic. There was a Civil War set in which the only merit of the blue and gray soldiers was their large number. I got more enjoyment from a set depicting

Custer's Last Stand. My favorite Indian was riding a horse and about to hurl a lance; but he had just been shot, his face was tilted heavenward, and you knew his lance would softly, uselessly, pierce the air. One of the bluecoats had an arrow in the belly, and he grasped the shaft with both hands as his head curled forward. Another trooper flung both hands into the air as an arrow drilled his back.

My brother was my principal playmate, but I played with my sister, too, at least until I was ten or so. With her the play was less rambunctious but just as imaginative. We had stuffed animals, plus dolls Jan had made out of old white socks, with hair of yarn and facial features inscribed in ink. Jan had a Barbie doll or something like it, but I wouldn't play with that. A boy has to draw the line somewhere. As you will see, however, my line had some remarkable indentations.

I had two bears: Bunkenhollow (a brown bear) and Pandy, whose name was generic. The rest of our menagerie belonged to my sister. Jan had a large red dog, Doggie Bon-Bon (wife of Pandy), whose zippered belly was large enough to contain smaller animals, her babies. Doggie Bon-Bon gave birth to Lambchops (the first-born, a black lamb), Tuffy (a gray dog), Pinky (another dog), and Shoebox (a chubby little brown dog who lived in a cardboard box). Jan manufactured sock-dolls named Mickey and Minnie McGillicuddy (a married couple) and the totally unrelated Lizzie. When my sister and I played with stuffed animals and dolls, we called ourselves the Mickey McGillicuddy Club. Bob refused to join.

Each of our creatures had a unique history and personality. Bunky was the patriarch of the clan, Pandy a lumbering dolt. Doggie Bon-Bon was an endlessly forgiving mother. Lambchops was a kind, honorable, protective big brother, like Jan and I thought Bob ought to be. Tuffy was a thug, always beating up everybody else. Lizzie was a woman of easy virtue. She often copulated with Tuffy but sometimes with Mickey or even Pandy, and she was always trying to seduce the other males. Jan and I were too uneducated to imagine homosexuality.

We featured our menagerie in comic books we created, with me as the writer and Jan as the artist. I wish we still had those homemade comics, but Mom threw them out during one of her moves from apartment to apartment after we left Oak Street. I donated my toy soldiers and baseball cards and store-bought comic books to the Shriners Hospital. That's a disadvantage of being poor: you move so often, and your apartments are so small, that you have no way to preserve items with only sentimental value. There is no attic or basement where memorabilia may repose for fifty years. Actually some of our possessions had value that was not merely sentimental: I had four Carl Yastrzemski rookie cards that predicted he would become a star. I was skeptical of all such promises. Oh, well. Bob and I played so much with our baseball cards that none of them was in anything close to mint condition. We had many shoeboxes full of cards but, unlike youths of the following generation, did not actually *collect* them. They were toys, not investments.

I also enjoyed forms of play that did not involve a toy or a game, at least not one with any rules—hiking, for example. With my friend Bryan or another boy—for some reason, these adventures usually involved exactly two people—I would walk west a few blocks, to where the city ended and the country began. After clambering down a long, steep, grassy hill, we would make our way to Hangman Creek.

In the summer the creek was shallow enough so we could find places to wade across. The valley through which it ran was home to a derelict vinegar factory whose odor was still detectable; numerous truck farms, including one owned by Bryan's Uncle Joe; empty stretches of parched earth where we lined up tin cans to plunk with BB and pellet guns; and railroad tracks that shot down the valley carved ages ago by the stream.

Spokane was a rail hub, and the trains provided endless entertainment. Sometimes we would place pennies on the rails, then marvel at the flattened disks after a train rolled over them. Often we tried to count the cars as they rumbled by, but our minds would wander and we would lose track before reaching a hundred. In more daring moments we would creep through a long, dark tunnel and hope we would find our way out before a train came in to join us. We told ourselves that if one were to come along, we would hurl ourselves to the ground, as far as possible from the rail bed, pressing against the chilly concrete wall of the tunnel and soaking ourselves in the stagnant water there. As luck would have it, we never had to implement that plan.

The Game Game

One day, though, I was meandering along the tracks, stopping and stooping to examine rocks and wildflowers and the litter that always seemed to accumulate there. I must have been engrossed in the objects at hand, because I did not hear or see anything else until I felt the ground shiver as a locomotive roared past, not ten feet from me. It was fortunate I had been strolling alongside the track instead of, as I sometimes did, between the rails. Delight and death were only a few steps apart.

Hangman Creek was no good for swimming: too turbulent if there had been heavy rains recently, and too shallow if there had not. We had other places to swim, though. Actually, *swim* might be too strong a word, since what I mainly did was perturb the water rather than propel my body through it: more commotion than locomotion. Nobody in my family was a strong swimmer. Some of my friends in Boy Scouts did the Mile Swim, but I never got beyond the required minimum of a hundred yards. Along with my mother, brother, and sister, however, I enjoyed splashing in cool water on a hot day.

Sometimes we would go to a pool at a city park; but we had to take a bus to get there, and there was something dispiriting about the scorching concrete desert surrounding the swimming pool. Also you had to wade through a shallow basin of disinfectant—stop the spread of polio!—before you could jump into the larger, deeper pool of diluted chlorine. The crowd at the swimming pool always included some idiot you didn't even know, who would do a cannonball dive into your kidney.

A lake was better. There we mostly played in water shallow enough for us to stand, but sometimes we ventured above our heads. Bob and I would have contests to see who could hold his breath longer underwater. I seldom won. I would look up at the wave-dimmed sun, then down at the murky, indeterminate floor; and although I knew I had been underwater for only a few seconds and my lungs held plenty of oxygen, a panic would start my arms and legs frantically pulling my body toward the light until I crashed into the free air and exhaled with violence, jubilant at my deliverance.

People in the East, where I live now, are often surprised when I tell them there is no ocean near Spokane. The Pacific is almost three hundred miles away, which means that I never went into it, except once when I fell off a raft into frigid Puget Sound. I didn't begin to get familiar with the sea until after I had moved to coastal Massachusetts, as a grown-up with a fully developed dread of deep water with distant shores. When I go swimming, I stay close to land and close to the surface, corraled and buoyed by visions of long-armed seaweed reaching up to drag me down.

My fear is partly the result of blindness. When in the water, I have to take off my glasses, which means I can see neither hazards in the sea around me, nor reassuring markers on land. That blur flashing beside me might be my wife, or it might be a great white shark. Once I dived off a boat and straight into a large red jellyfish, which I didn't see until it was draped across my shoulder. Deep water is where danger lives.

But that is now, and I should be telling you about long ago. In Spokane I played more on dry land than in water. One day, for example, Bob and I came home from school and discovered that a huge mound of dirt had miraculously appeared in the middle of our garden. We played King of the Mountain, clambering up the steep incline and trying to toss the other fellow aside. We sledded down on our bellies or skidded on our backs. When Mom came home from work, she stopped our play and ordered us to take long, thorough baths. She informed us that our mountain consisted of something called "manure." It must have been pretty dried-out, however, because it didn't smell too bad.

The cattle dung was for Mom's garden, which produced corn, cucumbers, potatoes, string beans, tomatoes, nasturtiums, wild rhubarb that we never ate, and, next to the water faucet, a solitary bush of raspberries. We kids helped with weeding and picking, but Mom did most of the work. For her, though, it was a form of recreation, where she could get a little exercise and quiet, away from both her job and her children.

Such escape was necessary. Mom still tells of the night she went to a PTA meeting where the teachers told her what bright, well-behaved children she had. When she came home, she found that Jan and I had Bob pinned on his back on top of the bunk bed he and I shared. He was cursing furiously, and it took all our strength and ceaseless vigilance to hold his writhing arms and legs in place. We had been in those positions for perhaps an hour. Jan and I knew that if Bob slipped loose, he would kill us, so we had to contain him until Mom came home. It was self-defense. Bob was always picking on us, but this night we had risen in rebellion. I guess I really didn't have to drool in his face while we held him down, but you take advantage of your opportunities when you have them.

Bob and I were inseparable, like Cain and Abel. I mean, you don't think of one without thinking of the other, do you? Once Bob used a rope to tie me to a chair. I was supposed to try to wriggle free. However, Bob amused himself by pulling on the loose end of the rope, tilting the chair further and further back on its hind legs, trying to find the balance point as I writhed in desperation. He tugged too far, and I crashed to the floor, banging the back of my head on the carpet.

I got even. One day as we walked home from the grocery store, he closed his eyes and impersonated a blind man as I gave him voice commands on which way to go. We got all the way to our back porch, and I walked him up the stairs. By the time he got to the top stair, I noticed he was at its right edge, three or four feet above the ground. Wouldn't it be funny, I thought, if he fell off? "One step right," I said. He took it and marched into the air.

He landed in a wooden wheelbarrow. By the time Mom came home from work, Bob was lying bloody and bruised on his bed. Fortunately for him, he had broken no bones. Fortunately for me, he was sufficiently damaged to seek no immediate vengeance.

As this episode shows, I have the ability to see myself as a character in a fiction—even in a comic strip or television cartoon—rather than an actual person whose deeds have real consequences. When I walked Bob off the stairs, it seemed to me like what Bugs Bunny would do to Elmer Fudd, or Beep-Beep the Road Runner to Wile E. Coyote.

A similar confusion between fantasy and life occurred one night several years later when my friend Tom and I were on our way home from a high school basketball game. Tom was walking on one side of the street and I, for some reason, on the other. There was a woman walking in front of me, and I thought it would be very funny for me to become her shadow, walking in her footsteps a single pace behind her. I did so, prancing in a manner that I considered sly and menacing, and looked at Tom, who stared back in disbelief. The woman I was following found nothing entertaining in the situation. She darted into a gas station, and through the glass wall I could see her gesticulating excitedly to the attendant. I fled the scene.

Tom and I had some more-harmless pastimes, such as Rok, spelled without the *c* that would have made the name tediously descriptive. This was a game we invented in eighth grade, after I had moved to Monroe Street, for walking the five blocks between Tom's house and Irving School. Each of us would select a stone about an inch across. It wasn't exactly round, but it couldn't be flat: it had to bounce. With the toe of your shoe, you would kick your rock toward your opponent's. You had to hit it to win; and with such an unevenly shaped ball, it usually took many tries to score a direct hit. On our way to school we sometimes had to declare the contest a draw, lest we be

167

late for class. On our way home, however, we always were able to finish the game. It's a pity that our later lives have not always had such an amplitude of time.

Nowadays I amuse myself by making a game of quotidian actions, turning necessity not into a virtue but something far better, a sport. When I have drained a twelve-ounce aluminum can of club soda, for example, I do not simply drop it into the recycling bin. Instead, I carry it down the hallway and open the door leading to the basement. When I flip on the light at the top of the stairs, I see at the bottom a tall, blue, rectangular clothes hamper with its lid flung open. The hamper, however, is not for laundry. I brace myself, my left foot slightly forward of my right, the can in my right hand, held down and back as if I were about to pitch a softball. I launch the can so it almost touches the down-sloping ceiling overhanging the stairs, but then falls softly into the hamper's wide mouth, sometimes directly, sometimes after bouncing off the gray drywall. "Two points!" I holler in triumph. Admittedly, I sometimes miss, and I then have to retrieve the can from where it has rolled, beneath the stairs. A one- or two-liter plastic bottle is harder to aim, floating and bouncing unpredictably, so it counts for three points.

When I shoot hoops in the driveway, I warm up with jump shots, hook shots, and layups. This helps the pedometer in my pants pocket click up to ten thousand steps per day—the quota I gleaned from a newspaper story about the health benefits of walking. But the desire for exercise isn't what keeps me out there. After the warmups comes the real event, the part I put in the record books: the free throws. I shoot a series of ten, then write down the number I scored. At the end of each month, then each year, I calculate my percentages. This produces statistics like the ones I used to study on the backs of baseball cards. In my first year of shooting free throws, I made 42 percent. I gradually got better, scoring in the 50s, then 60s, and in the last couple years I've made it into the low 70s. Neighbors walking by sometimes cheer when I make a basket, and I tell them I'm almost ready for the pros.

In view of the fact that I have spent my entire life playing games, it is perhaps surprising that I have never gotten good at any of them. Of course, I cannot expect to excel in athletics: my defective foot and eyes alone would prevent it, even without the clumsiness of the rest of my body. I gave only the briefest of trials to golf, tennis, pool, and bowling, then gave up. I never attempted to ski or surf. I have a dart board in the basement that I used to use when my wife invited her business associates to our house for a Christmas party, and I threw as accurately as could be expected from somebody who played once a year.

Some games, like the one with baseball cards that Bob and I invented, depend entirely on luck, so it is impossible to develop expertise. But what of the others—chess, bridge, pinochle, poker—games requiring mental skills, not physical ones? Why have I not become proficient in any of these? I have never competed in a bridge tournament. I have played blackjack many times at casinos, but only twice have I walked away from the table a winner. Why am I, after half a century of practice, still a beginner?

I admit that, in part, it's just because I'm lazy: I am unwilling to subject myself to the hard discipline and sustained exertion required to succeed. I admit as well that I do not possess extraordinary natural talent: how can I count cards, points, or trumps with a memory as feeble as mine? But I think the explanation is larger than all that. When I fail to develop skill in a game, it is in part because I don't think the game important enough to go to the trouble of developing a skill. In other words, I don't want play to become a form of work.

Don't get me wrong: when I'm playing a game, I like to win and I hate to lose. I may not care whether I ever possess much ability, but that doesn't mean I'm indifferent to success in the contest in which I am currently engaged. Whether it's pinochle with my mother and brother or a free-throw shooting contest against the young man next door, I show no mercy. Sometimes I have tried to let opponents win, but something inside me rebelled against such kindness: to me it seems a sin to lose a trick deliberately or aim a free throw at the clanking rim instead of the sweetly silent net. So, yes, I very much enjoy winning and I try to do so.

It's just that I am unwilling to work at it. For me, play is a matter of only the moment, and success is not a reward but a gift. That's why we call it "play."

Chapter Eight

❄ 𝔑𝔦𝔤𝔥𝔱𝔥𝔞𝔴𝔨𝔰 𝔞𝔫𝔡 𝔏𝔬𝔟𝔰𝔱𝔢𝔯𝔰 ❄

I shall tell you of my loves. Not all of them, to be sure: you have no need for a catalogue raisonné of amatory fiascos, numberless variations on a single disaster. No, a sampling will suffice.

But first a word about love, or at least a word about the word. If, as Lear taught us, *never* is the longest word in the English language, then *love* must be the largest, for it contains so many meanings. When I tell you of my loves, you may say of them, That is not love at all! This one is childish fantasy; that one, animal lust; this, ephemeral infatuation; and only that—that one there—the real thing, and maybe not even that. You may think I was never in love at all, except with love itself.

I shall not quarrel. I confess I know little of love: what is genuine and what is not, what are its different forms, how it starts and how it ends, how fervid it must be to be called love at all. I claim no more expertise in love than in basketball. So when I tell you of my love, I am only telling what seemed like it to me. Smile if you like, smirk if you must, but please do not interrupt.

Can a twelve-year-old be in love? If so, I was in love with Marlene. That was her real name, though the boys all called her Snookie. She had curly blonde hair and a square but cute face, and her breasts were high up on her torso. Once when she was sitting on the concrete steps at the entrance to Washington Irving Elementary School, I looked up her skirt and saw ruffled white knickers that came down almost to her knees. That was a fashion at the time—the knickers, I mean. She had a good singing voice, though a little nasal, with a timbre hinting of some fine metal. Along with Roxy, my assigned partner in square dancing class, she sang "Scarlet Ribbons" at the school talent show. I once gave Marlene a valentine that cost an entire dollar, practically a day's earnings from my paper route. She did not acknowledge receiving it.

But who could blame her? My attentions were not coveted by the girls. Once the school had a fund-raising dinner, and one girl and one boy were assigned as server and busboy at each table. My partner was Karen, with whom I had always gotten along amicably. Just before the dinner, I happened to be walking, invisible as usual, behind a gaggle of girls chatting about their partners. Somebody asked Karen who was hers. "Ohhhh," she replied in a drawn-out groan, "Ji-i-i-im." Some of the girls muttered their sympathy, while others chortled with malicious glee. I slowed up and let them walk away.

When I got to high school, I found more girls, different girls, a whole new world crowded with opportunities for frustration. The principal cause of that frustration was named Kathy.

Kathy was perhaps an inch shorter than I was but, unlike me, slender and athletic; she played on the tennis team. Her hair was dark and short, enveloping her head like a soft, round helmet. I thought her eyes were green, but later she told me they were hazel. Her face was the most expressive one I have ever seen, the eyes squinting for a moment, then flashing wide; the lips puckering in a pout, then twisting with the right corner curled higher than the left; then the whole mouth bursting open in a laugh. Her cheeks and forehead, always in motion, seemed made of rubber. Her face mirrored her mind, instantly registering perplexity, amazement, glee, disgust, sorrow, and, most commonly, delight. She concealed nothing.

What is it that makes a face beautiful? We can often agree that a visage is lovely or handsome, but we have a hard time stipulating exactly what makes it so. Of course it cannot have a double chin or horse teeth or a nose like a lightbulb or skin peppered with crimson craters from exploded pimples; but, aside from ruling out such obvious defects, you'll find it difficult to produce a formula for beauty. You could say, for example, that features should be regular and balanced, but there are plenty of homely people with evenly proportioned eyes and mouth. I cannot say, then, what made Kathy cute, but everybody said she was. In later years I would call her beautiful. Her face, especially the eyes and the corners of the mouth, would remind me of Elizabeth Taylor in *The Taming of the*

Shrew, though maybe that was just because by then she was calling herself "Kate."

Kathy was in my homeroom for all four years of high school; and, indeed, it is probably only because both our last names began with the same letter—the alphabet determined homeroom assignments—that I got to know her at all. Teachers often seated students alphabetically, so when Kathy and I took the same course, we sat near each other. Perhaps it was because we happened to be side by side in Debate class that she asked if I would like to be her partner for the next contest. I did not disguise my astonishment and joy. We prepared arguments pro and con over whether the United States should pursue a "more aggressive foreign policy." This was 1964, when Americans were beginning to hear about a place called Vietnam.

Debate class is an odd place to fall in love, but that's how it happened—for me, that is. Kathy and I went downtown to the Spokane Public Library, checked out old issues of *Newsweek* and *The Congressional Record*, and filled four-by-six-inch index cards with penciled data which, while true, were not the truth. We would use one set of cards to argue the affirmative, another set for the negative. As a debater, you learn to occupy two mutually exclusive universes and to function happily in either one. I suppose that some people learn from this that there are two sides to every question, but I suspect that more learn that you *win* by denying half of reality. There are lots of people who go through life with only one set of index cards.

174

Nighthawks and Lobsters

One day, as an intermission from research at the library, I took Kathy to a restaurant nearby and treated her to a hamburger and a Coke. This was as close as I got to a date with her in high school.

In my junior year I set a trap. As the newly elected class president, I initiated production of the Junior Con, a talent show. Kathy volunteered to help with the convocation, so I appointed her chairman of the Script Committee, even though she protested that she was unqualified to serve in that capacity. In an even grosser abuse of executive power, I named myself to that committee. Whenever it met, I luxuriated in Kathy's smiles.

She didn't spend any more time than necessary in my presence, however. One morning, during a rehearsal for the Con, I saw her watching from the front row. I said, "Mind if I sit next to you?"

"I don't care," she replied.

I thought about that for a moment, then sat three seats away.

The Con was performed twice during the day for the students, then once at night for their parents. After the evening performance I was standing next to Kathy when her mom and dad walked up. She did not introduce us.

I asked her out several times that year, but she was always busy. At the Christmas Mixer, however, I got my chance. Spotting her alone for a moment, I asked for a dance, and she consented. But when that was over and I asked for the next dance, too, she seemed bewildered. As the music blared, and I pumped my arms up and down in personification of a dance called The Jerk, Kathy looked around anxiously, like a mouse in a maze, sometimes stopping her bodily movement altogether while she searched for a route of escape. At the instant the music ended, she bolted from the floor. I vainly waited half an hour for her to reappear, then walked home in the quiet night, leaving the music behind.

Because of her I memorized all the lyrics to the Everly Brothers' song "Cathy's Clown." "Don't you think it's kinda sad that you're treatin' me so bad," I whined to myself nasally and off-key, "or don't you even care?"

I guess she had already answered that question. By our senior year I had given up on Kathy. She was dating a handsome blond boy who lived on the South Hill and played forward on the varsity basketball team. I think he took her to the Senior Prom, but I don't know for sure, because I wasn't there.

I wasn't at a lot of social events. It's true that I was busy: I worked six nights a week, so had only one left open for dating. That, however, proved to be one more than I needed. During my four years of high school, I dated three girls, none of them more than once.

The common nighthawk gave voice to my solitude. I didn't get off work until 10:30, and as I walked home, I would hear the nighthawks' terse screech echoing above the empty streets of the city. I suppose the male birds were just showing off to the females or trying to scare the other males away, but to me their cry seemed like the saddest sound in the world. It was not without beauty, however.

Nighthawks and Lobsters

At the end of our last year in high school, Kathy gave me a photo of herself. On the back she wrote in a precise hand, thanking me for having been a good friend and saying she admired my sense of humor. "Maybe we can get together sometime," she concluded.

What?

What was that she said? Maybe we can *get together*?

We have spent four years in the daily propinquity of homeroom, two of them with me continuously besieging the fortress of her affections; over the long and lonely years she has invented a thousand different ways to repel my forays; and after all that, as we leave our common school and go our separate ways in the vast and various world, now she says that maybe we can *get together*?

It actually happened. Kathy and I grew closer after we left for college, she to Seattle, Washington, and I to Providence, Rhode Island. This was when I discovered that I get along well with women as long as we're three thousand miles apart. My friend Tom, who went to the same university as Kathy, reported to me that she had changed. After our freshman year, Kathy and I were both home in Spokane for the summer.   I called her and asked for a date, and she said yes. She had, indeed, changed.

She didn't want to be called "Kathy" anymore. She associated that name with the person she used to be or at least had seemed to be: the innocent, the church-goer, the Girl Scout. But now she was different. Now she was "Kath" or "Kathryn." Often she used no first name at all but only her last. In later years she would sometimes be "Kate." "Kathy," however, was dead.

We got together several times that summer, for lunch, coffee, a picnic in the park. Often we talked about what we had done and learned in college. I believe it was at this time, though it may have been a few years later, that she told me of her enthusiasm for Ayn Rand. Kathryn said that you should simply, honestly do what you want, not worrying about what other people want you to do. I agreed with that up to a point, but—perhaps with an earnestness she found sanctimonious—I also said you need to take other people's interests and feelings into account. She said that would be like walking on eggshells, an impossible task. I said you had to try. One evening many years later I tried to read Rand's novel *Atlas Shrugged* but, after sixty-six pages of prose that made me think of rigor mortis, I shrugged, skipping the last thousand pages. The strange thing was that while I was on page fifty-six, reading about "clean, hard, radiant competence," Kathryn called to say hello.

Once during that magical summer of 1968 Kathryn looked at me and said, without an impish smile, without a trace of irony, "You're beautiful." I realized that something odd had happened. Kathryn had changed. The English language had changed. The world had changed. The only thing that hadn't changed was me.

One day I picked up Kathryn in my Chevrolet Corvair—with bucket seats and "four on the floor"—and took her on a picnic at Riverside State Park. It was raining, so we ate our lunch in the shelter of a cave—a shallow niche scooped out of basalt eons ago by the Spokane River in its turbulent youth. When the rain decayed into a drizzle, we got back into the Corvair and went for a ride. We followed the river on its winding course, then parked beneath the trees where we could watch the water rushing by, at least until the windows fogged. Kathryn was telling me of arguments with her mother about religion, morality, life. Once, she said, she had run out of the house in desperation but then realized she had nowhere to go. Now she softly cried. In my memory her tears are forever blended with the river and the rain.

I wanted to pull her to me, hold her, comfort her, and do a good deal else besides. But I did not. There was, I discovered, a great disadvantage to a car with bucket seats and a stick shift on the floor between them. I wished I were driving Uncle Fred's Buick LeSabre with its long bench-seat in front. I suppose I could have reached across the hard white ball atop the gearshift lever and tried to grasp Kathryn's hand, but I did not. She had warded off my touch before, and now I feared that if I reached for her, she would stiffen and recoil, saying that was not what she wanted, that was not it at all. So I did nothing.

Kathryn finished her story and dried her eyes. I turned the key to arouse the engine and drove on. It would not be for another nine years, at our ten-year high school reunion, that Kathryn and I would finally kiss; and even that was only momentary, as we were saying good-night.

We saw each other every now and then, but—since we ended up living on opposite sides of the continent—more often wrote letters or made phone calls. I wrote and called more than she did. Year after year I sent what I came to call "unrequited birthday cards"; once she asked me why I knew her date of birth but she did not know mine. She apologized for not writing more often but explained that she hadn't felt like writing or else she felt like writing but couldn't find the right words. But then, when she hadn't written in two or three years and I had given up on her forever, the phone would ring. Once she mailed me a loaf of banana bread, which I treasured but nevertheless ate.

Kathryn was a seeker. One year she dropped acid. The next, she found the Lord. She worked for a while as the business manager for an underground newspaper, until she discovered that underground newspapers don't operate like a business. Even after she took a job in the straight world, however, she managed to get to the Taj Mahal, and she told me all about it.

Once Kathryn and I staged an experiment in mental telepathy. We arranged that on a certain evening, at a certain hour and minute, she would try to communicate with me through thought alone. At the appointed moment, I ceased all activity and tried to empty my mind, to make way for a transmission from Kathryn. I waited for a word, a voice, an image, an idea. But there was nothing. Nothing at all.

As usual.

Kathryn and I had different tastes. She wrote poems that made no sense to me; and when I recited Chaucer, she clapped her hands over her ears and ran away.

We had some things in common, though. One day Kathryn was describing to me how she had taken LSD for the first time and had ingested ten times the normal dosage. I interrupted her narrative by exclaiming, "Wow!" She looked at me intently. "You know," she said quietly, "that's *our* word."

It's a children's word, of course, one of discovery and amazement. I remember using it when confronting all sorts of bright reality: a waterfall, Shakespeare, napalm.

Nighthawks and Lobsters

People of our generation—not everybody, of course, but a great many—said Wow! all the time and still do. It's a child's prayer.

When Kathryn told me she was getting married, I told her good-bye. Why? she asked, surprised. The men in her life had never come between her and me before, she said; why should they now? She said she needed me as a friend. A couple years later she got divorced. She told me that a woman needed to get married in order to prove to herself that some man had been willing to marry her. After that, though, she had no need for a husband. In following years Kathryn would tell me of her boyfriends: a firefighter, a marine, and other manly men: the kind who rode motorcycles. I never even learned to ride a bicycle.

Sometimes I would try to persuade her that perhaps, just for variety, she should try somebody different, somebody like me. I pointed out that each of us had bought a Chevy Corvair, then later a Honda Civic hatchback (white); and didn't those choices reveal a profound compatibility between us? Weren't cars more important than politics, religion, and poetry? I didn't realize that when choosing a mate, you choose someone with certain preferences the opposite of yours, which is why that person often belongs to what is called the opposite sex.

Kathryn would set me straight. She said that if, somehow, we were to try to make a go of it, she would "eat me alive." Once she wrote me a letter saying that although she found me "extremely interesting," her attraction to me was not of the "traditional man/woman" type. I must have replied that my attraction to her was more traditional, because Kathryn in her next letter explained to me that my basic problem was that I didn't know what to do with women, and that was one of the reasons why she and I would never be anything more than "friends."

She was right, of course. I even have a photograph proving it. Once, on vacation in Alaska, I went to a saloon where every male customer had his picture taken with a dancehall girl. The young woman stands on my left, both of us smiling at the camera, though her lips are invitingly open and mine nervously pursed. Her right hand reaches behind my back and rests on my right shoulder, while my left arm disappears behind her until my fingertips emerge and gingerly touch her waist. Her left hand pulls the hem of her golden gown above her left thigh as she kicks that leg up and out in front of me, waist-high, bent slightly at the knee; and it is obvious that I am supposed to support her shapely leg in its black, fishnet stocking by cupping my right hand under her calf or knee. Obvious, that is, to everybody but me. In the five-by-seven color photograph I bought for ten dollars, my right arm hangs uselessly by my side, and the dancehall girl must depend on her own strength alone to suspend her forsaken leg in the empty air.

Kathryn did not despise me, though—not yet. She used to tell me how much she treasured my friendship. She said she needed to write and talk to me; she needed me to listen. She said that several times I had kept her from going crazy. She said I should not be surprised if someday she should show up on my doorstep. I imagined what I would say to her that day: Welcome home.

She never did appear at my door. Instead, we had a falling out that was sudden and complete.

One night Kathryn told me on the phone about a new job and a new boyfriend. A month later I called to wish her Merry Christmas but found she had changed to an unlisted phone number, so I sent a card wishing her the very best in the new year. Shortly after that I got a letter from her, accusing me of betrayal.

I had no idea what she was talking about, so I wrote back and asked what I had done. I also asked for her new phone number, but she never gave it to me. Thus she controlled a valve on our communication: I could not call her, but she could call me whenever she chose. One night, she chose. She explained that in our previous conversation I had shown no enthusiasm for either her career or her lover: I had not wanted to talk about them, not wanted to listen. I admitted she may have been half right, but no more than half, and maybe not even that much. If I was abrupt with her (and I didn't remember being so), perhaps it was because I was tired: if it was 10 p.m. in her time zone, it was 1 a.m. in mine—her phone calls often woke me up. She said no, that wasn't it, I was her enemy, I wanted her to fail at everything. *That* I denied. She said I was a false friend, a traitor. I said that if she couldn't treat me more kindly than she was now doing, then maybe we should end our friendship. She said, Fine! I have not seen or spoken to her since.

I dream of her, though, every now and then. In some dreams we're breaking up, walking away from one another, and that makes me wake up feeling sad. In other dreams, we're getting back together, hugging, laughing. That makes me sadder still.

Kathryn was the only woman I ever loved who dispatched me from her life with rancor. Most have done so with either compassion or indifference, though sometimes it is hard to tell which. Take Randi, for example.

I met Randi in the summer after my sophomore year of high school. I took a train to Salem, Oregon, and Willamette University—"It's Wil-LAM-ette, DAMN-it!" is how they taught us to pronounce the name of the school—for a two-week "institute" on Communications Arts and Sciences. (I wanted to be a journalist.) Randi was there for a related institute for Junior Engineers and Scientists. (She wanted to be a horticulturist like her father.) I don't know whether Randi lived on an actual farm, but her mailing address was on a Rural Route in a town in Oregon that was too small to have its own high school, so she had to travel each day to an adjacent town.

At the two summer institutes at Willamette, the combined student body consisted of twenty boys and a hundred forty girls, which was why I was able to spend many hours in the presence of someone as desirable as Randi. (Perhaps I should have remembered this when I applied to colleges.) I fell in love instantly, despite the fact that I was already in love with Kathy. Did I ever claim that my love was exclusive?

I corrupted Randi—at least, that was our joke. What it meant was that in evenings after class I taught her to play poker. "Pasteboards of the Devil!" I proclaimed as I slapped down the cards for stud or draw. In the coming months I would enclose in each letter I sent her a solitary Queen of Hearts. She would protest that I was spending too much money on cards.

Not that we ever had an actual date. Our poker games included whatever kids happened to be around: I don't think I was ever alone with Randi. Still, this did not stifle my imagination. When the summer institute ended, I was picked up by some old friends of my mother who lived in Salem. As their car sped down the freeway, taking me to their home for a brief visit before I would get on the train that would take me back to Spokane, I spotted Randi in a car we were passing. Randi and I waved at each other excitedly. What kind of coincidence was this? Surely it portended something wonderful! Destiny, I believed, had something in store for us.

I never saw her again.

She did write to me, however, in a small, neat hand on perfumed yellow paper. I inhaled every letter. She said that I was one of the most wonderful people she knew and that seeing me in a passing car on the freeway had made her feel happy all the way home. She said she missed all the fun we had had at Willamette. Why, she asked, did all good things have to come to an end? At Willamette we had talked about the word *nostalgia*, its etymology and meaning; and now, she said, my letters brought her happy memories and nostalgia. It was, Randi reminded me more than once, a good word.

In time, however, I came to distinguish between nostalgia and grief, believing there was something meretricious about the former. Nostalgia is what you feel for what you have left behind; grief is what you feel for what has been taken away.

When Randi was a senior in high school and I a junior—did I mention that she was older than me?—I asked for a copy of her graduation picture. She said she would send me one, but forgot. The next October I got a letter postmarked Palo Alto, California, and learned from it that Randi had gotten a full scholarship to Stanford. I asked again for her photo, and she said she would get one for me the next time she went home, but she never did send it.

After reading one of my letters, Randi told me I sounded depressed. That surprised her, she said, because at Willamette I had always been cheerful and full of fun. I pointed out that when she had seen me at Willamette, I had always been with her.

Randi's letters grew less and less frequent. I would have to send two or three messages to provoke her into sending one. She apologized profusely, abjectly, repeatedly, for not writing sooner. Finally, though, her letters ceased altogether. I gathered all I had received, wrapped them with rubber bands, and stored them in a cardboard box. For years I could smell the perfume, but finally it dissipated.

Nighthawks and Lobsters

Randi did not vanish, however—not altogether. Once in a while, every few years, I'll dream of her. The problem is that I don't know what she looks like. Of course, I have no idea how she looks now, half a century after I saw her face in the window of a car slowly melting into the distance on an Oregon highway. But I don't even remember how she looked back then. I recall she was pretty and blonde, but there are a million different ways to be pretty and blonde. No matter how hard I try, I can't remember her face, and I have no photograph to remind me. In my dreams I see her, and I know it's she. When I wake up, I try to hold onto that image, but it dissolves and disappears, and I am left with nothing. All I have of Randi is a memory of a memory.

Once I dreamt that Randi and I were riding on the beach in a dune buggy on a trail through the sand to the sea. She was driving, of course; I can't drive a dune buggy even in my dreams. We stopped at the water's edge and stared into an opaque silver mist where the ocean should have been.

A few months later a long-lost buddy from childhood rediscovered me through the World Wide Web, and he introduced me to the art of Googling. I looked up so many people, some men but mostly women, that my computer started receiving advertisements from dating services.

One of the people I looked up was Randi, and I found her. I sent her an e-mail, and she e-mailed back. We talked about our careers: how I had become a historian instead of a journalist, while she had become a journalist instead of a horticulturist. Funny how these things work out. I wrote to her again and then again, and she wrote back. I sent her a copy of my first book, pointing out a passage about nostalgia and grief, a passage inspired by the correspondence between Randi and me decades before. She did not acknowledge receiving the book, so I asked if my disparagement of nostalgia had hurt or offended her. She said no, she was sorry for not writing, but she had been very busy and had had time only to skim the book. I thanked her for writing back and said I looked forward to the next message from her. I never got another.

Biography repeats itself. The first time it's history; the second time, farce. The third time, it's just me.

Poly, pretty Poly, Poly of the single ell! You were my first girlfriend and very nearly my last. *Your* face I remember, even your street address in Brockton. Your full name was Polyna—Puh-LEE-nuh—Lithuanian, you explained—and I thought its oddity appealing. To me, any girl seemed exotic, but this one especially so.

Poly—spelled with one ell but pronounced like any double-elled Polly—Poly was desperate when I met her. It was our second semester in college, and Spring Weekend was upon us. This was the grandest social event of the year: the entertainers included Flip Wilson, Dionne Warwick, the James Brown Revue, the Yardbirds, Procol Harum, Ian and Sylvia, Dizzy Gillespie, Lawrence Ferlinghetti, Allen Ginsberg. Then, of course, there were all the parties. Poly wanted to go but did not have a date. One of her friends knew one of my friends, and our friends set up Poly and me for the weekend. It was my first date in college. Some of the guys in my dorm ran down the hallway yelling, "Hijiya's gone hetero! Hijiya's gone hetero!"

Poly had a wave of light brown hair cascading down each side of her head, with the curled tip of each inverted wave almost reaching her chin. Unlike most of the students at our cosmopolitan university, she had a full-blown Yankee accent that I found charming. She bragged, though, that she was from Massachusetts, not a dinky, insignificant state like Rhode Island.

Her father was a lobsterman, and in the summer Poly built the wooden traps he used. Lobsters had been hard to find in Spokane, Washington, at least if you were poor, so I knew nothing about them: neither the dusky ones scuttling in silence across the ocean floor, nor the bright red ones motionless astride a platter. Poly told me that someday she would teach me the proper way to eat a lobster, but she never got around to it. When she and I went out to dinner, we never ordered that dish. She ate it all the time at home for free, so why pay lots of money for it in a restaurant? It would be years before I would learn, through bibbed trial and buttery error, how to handle this crustacean.

One night when Poly and I were walking home from a play, I performed the most romantic gesture of my life. We were in the rain—why are so many of my sweetest memories associated with water?—and we stopped on a bridge over the Providence River. Today that waterway is elegantly reminiscent of the canals of Venice, with torchlight and gondolas, thanks to urban revival led by a mayor who later was imprisoned. In 1968, however, the river was a sluggish drain of stinking filth. But on that drizzly spring night, as I held Poly's hand and stopped on the bridge and drew her to me in her powder-blue raincoat and kissed her, that river was the Seine.

We walked on, preparing for the climb up College Hill, when we came to a large puddle. We stopped, I looked at it, I looked at her, then suddenly I swept my left arm under her knees, my right arm behind her back, picked her up, and, sloshing up to my ankles in the black water, carried her across the puddle and returned her to her feet on the opposite side, to be rewarded with a huge smile and another kiss. Fortunately Poly was slender, easy to carry, and I was exalted.

Unfortunately the school year ended, and Poly announced she was not coming back in the fall. She disliked college and was applying for VISTA—Volunteers in Service to America—the domestic Peace Corps. That summer I had a job in Spokane, so Poly and I kept in touch through letters. Her handwriting was large and round, which I thought accorded with her name, with all its loops and circles: roly poly. Cursive in the extreme, even her ell looked oval.

Poly said she loved my letters, the way I used language. This is a recurrent theme in my life. Kathryn told me she loved my words. Randi said she loved to get letters from me, though she added that it really didn't need to be quite so often. Many years later another friend of mine would tell me she would rather get a letter from me than see me in person.

Whenever a woman says something like this, I try to take it as a compliment, but I can't help remembering the courtship of Miles Standish. You may recall that in that tale invented by Longfellow, the Pilgrim captain was in love with a maid named Priscilla. The old soldier was oafish with language, so he sent his lieutenant, well-spoken John Alden, to do his courting for him. When the young man presented his captain's proposal, however, Priscilla famously asked, "Why don't you speak for yourself, John?" He did so, and Priscilla responded by marrying John. So when Poly told me she loved my words, I felt like Miles Standish.

After school resumed in September, Poly visited me in Providence and I visited her in Brockton. One evening she said she would show me her father's boat on Long Island. I thought her father must have an awfully long daily commute from Brockton to Long Island, but I discovered that Long Island was somewhere near Boston, connected to the mainland by a bridge. That dark night Poly and I strolled in the sand, holding hands and talking. We huddled on the beach, in the cool air under the icy stars and frozen moon, and it was there that I lost something precious.

At least I *think* I lost it there. When I got home that night, I realized that my hip pocket was empty. I called Poly the next morning, and she said she would look for my wallet at the beach. Alas, she never found it; maybe the tide took it along with our footprints in the sand.

During that fall semester Poly decided to come back to school. She had been rejected by VISTA—they said she was too young and lacking in practical skills—and had started to miss being in college. She had forfeited her scholarship by dropping out, but by living at home and waitressing at two restaurants she had saved enough money to pay the tuition for the second semester. She told me that she thought of me every day and couldn't wait to see me. When the new term started at the end of January, I welcomed her back joyfully, but our romance did not see another spring.

We had a date on Valentine's Day. I showed up at her dorm with a fistful of flowers, but she wasn't there. I guess that was a bad sign, but how was I supposed to know? A few weeks later we had a date for the theater. She came to my room but then told me she didn't want to go out with me anymore. She went back to her dormitory, and I went to the play. I don't remember what it was— Pinter, maybe—but I remember staring at the empty seat beside me.

That night I discovered the analgesic properties of literary composition. I couldn't sleep, so I got up and wrote a poem. I scribbled all night, then typed it out in the light of day.

Nighthawks and Lobsters

"I guess you know already what I have
to say." She didn't turn to look at him.
She knew that he had sensed it, too. And yet
he said, "I don't. What is it?" hoping that
it might have only been about a thing
he'd done, or hadn't.

You can tell, perhaps, that I had been reading Robert Frost. The poem went on for two and a half pages but grew so feeble that I never bothered to memorize the rest.

Whatever the degree of its literary merit, my poem was therapeutic or at least anesthetic. As I wrote it, and for a day or two thereafter, my sadness over losing Poly was mixed with a trace of elation, the happiness you feel when art makes you see. The man in my poem was not I but someone upon whom I could look with compassion. The sorrow was real, but it wasn't mine.

I thought I didn't love Poly, at least not much. She had never swept me off my feet, knocked me head over heels, or subjected me to any other such state of conventional ecstasy—not like Kathy or Randi. I thought I would get over losing her, I would find myself another girlfriend. As it turned out, I was right—I got another girlfriend. What I did not realize, however, was that it would take eighteen years.

During my last two years of college I did not see Poly—we must have moved in different circles. In my senior year, however, I went to the university housing office and got her address. (In those innocent days, when campus cops did not carry guns, universities freely

195

dispensed such intimate information.) I called on her, and we chatted. She told me that because she had dropped out of school temporarily, she would graduate one semester behind me.

Shortly before my own Commencement, I couldn't sleep. Sometime before dawn, I crept out of my apartment, as my housemates slumbered, and slunk down the dark streets to Poly's. I stood on the sidewalk and looked up at her house, wondering if she were even home. Trapped in the white glare from a streetlamp, I was a clown on stage before an empty house, with nothing to say or no way to say it. I wondered what Poly would do if she looked out her window and saw me standing there. Call the cops? I left.

I saw her later that day. I was part of the cap-and-gowned procession wriggling like a great black caterpillar down College Hill to the Baptist Meeting House for the baccalaureate service; and I saw Poly, a spectator, strolling on the sidewalk. We exchanged quick hellos, but she did not stop to say good-bye. When I got home, I clipped her photo from a yearbook and hid it in my wallet.

Poly is the last of the girls about whom I still dream. I call them girls because they were teen-agers when I met them, and in my dreams they still are. Dreams are a form of memory. Once I dreamt that a colleague of mine told me he had seen Poly shelving books in the library. This dream made no sense to me—what did Poly have to do with a library? A few years later I dreamt I saw her sitting behind a desk at a library, but she told me she was not a librarian. Again I could not explicate the dream. It was not until more years had passed and I re-read ancient letters Poly had sent me that I was reminded she had worked in a library in the summer after dropping out of college. My dreams remembered what my waking mind did not.

I believe in dreams.

I dream of Poly more than Randi but less than Kathy. But why do I dream so much of these three, whom I knew so little and so long ago? It's true that I dream mainly of people I knew in my youth: my mother, brother, and sister; uncles and aunts; neighbors in Spokane; buddies at college—I dream of them more than of people from the more recent past. My dream world is an airless, windless, lifeless white desert like the moon, where the footprints that an astronaut leaves in the dust will last forever, undisturbed. Still, why do I dream of Kathy, Randi, and Poly but not of Marlene and others of whom I soon shall tell? Is it love? Or just petrified caprice? As I told you, I have no understanding of matters such as this.

Breaking up with Poly did not put an end to my social life, but it came close. Sometimes I would draw up a list of women with whom I would like to go out, and I would call them one after another. No matter how long the list, however, it was sometimes too short to find me a date. Once, for example, I invited a woman from one of my classes to go with me to a performance by a tremendously popular band called Cream—you have heard of Eric Clapton. She said that unluckily she had another engagement that night, but she tried to encourage me by saying she was sure I would have no trouble finding a date for such an exciting event. I told her I wished she hadn't said that. At the concert, when everybody was jumping up and down and clapping and dancing, I had the convenience of depositing my coat on the empty seat beside me.

But why should I emphasize the negative? Let me tell you about the dates I *did* have. For instance, there was a beautiful woman named Jane whom I met on the bus. How, you may be wondering, did I find the nerve to start talking to a beautiful woman on the bus? Well, I didn't. I was talking to the driver. Lost as ever, I was asking him where I should get off, and Jane spoke up to inform me. We got to talking, and she told me she went to college in New Hampshire but was home in Providence on vacation. Before she got off the bus, she gave me her phone number. A few days later I invited her to a concert by Peter, Paul & Mary. I didn't have a car, but Jane said she would pick me up at school, outside the library. I asked what kind of car I should look for. She said a gold Cadillac. Her father was a dentist.

After the concert, we talked about literature. Jane said she wanted to read *The Lord of the Rings*. As it happened, I owned a boxed set of the three volumes, plus *The Hobbit*, all of which I had read during a previous semester's Study Week, when we were supposed to be preparing for final exams. I always resented finals, figuring that since I had already read the books and listened to the lectures, why should I have to think about them all over again?

Therefore, I would take my mind off exams by reading something like *The Lord of the Rings*. I never did very well on finals. Anyway, when Jane said she wanted to read Tolkien, I lent my copies to her.

I figured that if Jane borrowed my books, she would have to see me at least one more time in order to return them. Clever, no? A little exploitative, maybe; almost diabolical. Now, decades later, I can admit my selfish intent. And, Jane, if you're out there somewhere, I want you to know that I harbor no resentment or ill will toward you. You can keep the books.

Then there was my date with Judy, whom I had met at an art museum. I had discovered that lots of attractive young women, unaccompanied by men, were at museums—guys don't go there much. The women would be looking at paintings and sculptures; and I, a Visigoth in glasses, would be looking at the women. So I approached Judy, chatted with ignorant enthusiasm about art, and wangled a date. Judy went to a college nearby, and there was a special bus that ran between our two schools on weekends, so she came to see me.

I took her to an evening of one-act plays at the campus theater. One of the plays was a comedy about the death of God. I was the author, and I thought Judy might be impressed. After the show I brought her back to my room.

I had prepared. I had stocked up on wine and liquor, of course. I also had gone to the library and checked out record albums by Gerry Mulligan and Buddy Rich. Best of all, I had purchased a blue, forty-watt lightbulb that I screwed into the lamp on the table near the bed. What more could I do?

When we entered the room, I took Judy's coat. I offered her a drink, but she declined. She said she was tired. I suggested she lie down on my bed. I turned off the bright ceiling light and turned on the table lamp with the blue bulb. I pulled the Mulligan record from its jacket and, after some fumbling in the dark with the stereo, got the music to commence. I adjusted the volume, turned, approached the bed, and looked down at Judy.

She was asleep. Sound asleep. An evening of one-act plays written by undergraduates will do that to you sometimes. (The reviewer for the school paper said my play was "a rather boring joke.") I jiggled the bed with my fingers, but the sleeping beauty did not wake. I had never seen anyone other than my brother fall asleep so fast and so deep. I had plenty of time to study Judy, letting my eyes grow accustomed to the dim blue light. She had a pretty face, and her lips were opened slightly. She looked cold lying on top of the covers, so I got an extra blanket from the closet and spread it over her. Then I sat at my desk, turned on the fluorescent lamp there but bent its coiled neck down so the glare would not trouble the slumberer, and studied American history. When the proper time came, I shook Judy awake and walked her to the bus stop.

Maybe I should have tried the Buddy Rich. What do I know about jazz?

Nighthawks and Lobsters

In Ithaca, New York, where I went to graduate school for five years, then taught for two years at a college across town, I got into the habit of going on dates with a married woman. This was neither as good nor as bad as it sounds. Our friendship was warm but strictly chaste, though I confess that, on my part, moral principle was buttressed by the absence of encouragement to misbehave.

Jessica was a woman from New York City with long, dark hair. She had been a student of mine during my first semester as a teaching assistant. The following year I took her out once or twice, but nothing came of that. She graduated and got married, but then, a few years later, returned to Ithaca to pursue a master's degree while her husband toiled in New York. Her apartment was just a couple blocks down the street from mine.

We became dining companions. Sometimes I made dinner for her, sometimes she for me. Her husband was a vegetarian, so she enjoyed the opportunity I gave her to prepare and eat dishes with meat. In return she taught me to make an asparagus and cheese casserole that I would later serve to vegetarian guests.

Our most memorable meal was a picnic. I carried a basket that included a bottle of champagne. We walked far enough for the bottle to get thoroughly shaken; and when I popped the cork, the bubbly did not bubble but blasted—into the sky, all over our picnic blanket and ourselves, watering the lawn. We didn't get to drink much, but we had a day of laughter nevertheless. I shall forever associate Jessica with green grass and sunshine.

In later years there would be other women playing Jessica's role as "just a friend" with whom I would share supper; women who, all evening, would sit directly across a small table from me in a quiet restaurant or even in an apartment, but who nevertheless would remain infinitely beyond reach. And I would be what I always was: a kindly, funny little fellow, slightly tipsy as often as not, but withal harmless and inoffensive; almost—almost—a gentleman.

You seem a little fidgety. I know I have been talking a very long time. I detect a murmuring discontent, a complaint that something is missing. Is it sex you want? Is that what you've been waiting for?

Let me assure you that you have not waited as long as I. Your impatience is nothing compared to mine. Let us, then, fly rapidly over the Gobis and Saharas of my love life—decades of drought and blowing sand!—and parachute, as it were, into the cool green oasis known as Rachel.

You don't need to know much about Rachel: how I met her, when, or where. You don't need to know how she looked or what she did for a living. All you need to know is that late one winter's night Rachel and I sat at a bar, and she told me that two insurmountable barriers stood between us. First, she had a boyfriend whom she had no intention of leaving. Second, even if she were looking for a lover, she would never choose me.

At first I found this information discouraging. I was so depressed the next morning that, as I shoveled snow from the sidewalk, I found myself singing Neil Diamond songs. "You're not a dream, you're not an angel, you're a woman"—that's depressed. The following evening, however, I went out with Rachel again. You might think this persistence shows manly self-confidence and heroic determination. If so, however, you haven't been paying attention. What my perseverance actually reveals is that I never learn.

The evening started normally enough, with cocktails, then dinner with a bottle of wine at one of the finer restaurants in town. Then we went back to Rachel's house. She said she wanted to change into something more comfortable. While she did that, I uncorked a bottle of champagne.

Rachel came back to the den wearing blue jeans and a man's shirt. She then brought life to the fireplace, a rampant blaze that reminded me of bonfires in the Boy Scouts. In the Scouts, however, we did not have a couch on which we could sit while watching the dance of the flames. We also did not have the fifth of Johnny Walker Black that I had brought as an offering.

By the time we finished the champagne and the scotch, we had descended to the carpet and were sitting with our backs resting against the sofa's firm knee and our toes warming before the fire. Rachel got up, walked to another room, and came back with an already opened bottle of scotch. Before the night was over, that bottle was finished, too.

At this point, alas, my story begins to flicker, to start and stop like a poorly edited videotape with gaps of eighteen minutes, eighteen seconds, or an hour. Largely the problem lies in my memory. In the best of circumstances it's as incomplete as a slice of swiss cheese. Cocktails, wine, champagne, and a bottle and a half of scotch do not constitute the best of circumstances. Alcohol burns enormous holes in the fragile tissue of my recollection. On the other hand, without alcohol I might have nothing worth recollecting. Life is full of dilemmas such as this. But let us get back to our story.

The next scene I remember is of me lying on my back on the carpet with Rachel astride me and her bare breasts drooping toward my face. How we came to be in those positions I do not recall. I would like to think that it began with kissing, then subtly, gently, with an almost liquid grace, I slipped my warm hand up inside her shirt, sliding slowly across the pounding heart, under the cup of the bra, feeling the nipple beneath the tips of my fingers; that she unbuttoned her shirt herself and dropped it behind her, pulled down the straps of her brassiere, unhooked those tiny metal clasps connecting the two elastic bands in back, since I have never really gotten the hang of doing that, and flung the bra backhand across the room, not caring where it landed. This, as I said, is what I would like to think happened. Probably, however, it bears no relationship to what actually occurred. All I know for sure is that as I lay on my back with Rachel's nipples so close to my myopic eyes that I could see them with perfect clarity, even by the dim light of the diminishing fire, I very much enjoyed the spectacle.

I could describe what happened next. I could tell you of commands and eager acts of obedience; of ingenious contortions and languid bounces; of conversations conducted in a whisper. I could tell you fine details about how Rachel and I passed our long love's night, details that might startle and amuse.

But I shall not. There are some stories that should not be told.

When I awoke, I was freezing on the floor. The fire was out. Rachel, feeling the chill, had dressed herself again. I put on my clothes. When we reached the front door, we kissed. Then I walked out into the cold, gray morning.

I drove home and went straight to bed. When I awoke for the second time that day, my whole body ached, inside and out. I took a shower, and the hot water felt like a thousand needles jabbing my kneecaps. I looked down and, carefully examining both brightly red knees, discovered that patches of skin had been removed. I recalled that the carpet by the fireplace had been wiry and coarse, and this was when I realized how strenuously I had exerted myself in the fashion missionaries used to recommend. I taped a large bandage over each knee.

I wrote a letter to Rachel for each of the next four days. I told her I loved her, I wanted to live with her forever, I had never been so happy in my life.

She did not respond.

I called her and left messages on her answering machine, but she did not reply to them. Finally one day I phoned and caught her at home. She said she couldn't talk to me because her boyfriend was there. I called another night when he wasn't there. But this time, too, Rachel hung up on me.

Eventually I realized that what she had told me that night at the bar was true. The barriers between us were still insurmountable, and one long night in front of a fire had not changed a thing. My first love affair was a one-night stand.

But what a night.

Chapter Nine

✳ Ah-DAH! ✳

"J eemy says, 'Ah-DAH!'"

This was the observation of my cousin Dave, six months older than I and infinitely more articulate. Either he was fast in learning to talk, or I was slow. He reported my utterance to my mother, brother, and sister, and they laughingly repeated it for years to come. My first recorded attempt at speech had been an indecipherable iamb. Ah-DAH!

For me, it was a harbinger. The blurted word. The babble not understood. From the mouth of babes, speaking in tongues. The prophecy of language. The language of prophecy. Ah-DAH! Ah-DAH! Ah-DAH!

The first words I remember hearing and understanding were my mother's. She held me in her arms and stood by the light switch in the living room. I reached out my right hand and with my chubby fingers flipped the white plastic switch up and down. My mother announced, "Lie-tahn. Lie-toff. Lie-tahn. Lie-toff." This went on for quite some time, and we repeated it day after day.

At about this time Mom composed a verse for me and about me, and she recited it for several years:

> Jikkermody wodyho—
> He's the jodiest boy I know.
> That is why I love him so.
> You bet I do, you bet I do,
> I just love my
> Jikkerwicker hoyjoy,
> The poyjoy boyjoy woyjoy.

Mom changed the last two lines every time she spoke the poem. The meaning of the words didn't matter as much as the sound.

More than anybody else, my mother introduced me to language. Sitting on a bed, she would read aloud Bible stories from a big book she got as a Sunday School teacher. I still can see the walls of Jericho come tumbling down, a picture—a *moving* picture—conveyed by words alone. She also recited poetry, most memorably "The Rime of the Ancient Mariner," from a textbook she had saved from high school. She accented the alternating syllables as if she were hammering nails: "It *is* an *an*-cient *mar*-i-*ner*/ And he *stop*-peth *one* of *three*." It was that rhythmic exaggeration, perhaps, that made me recognize poetry as something out of the ordinary, and the iamb is the only metrical foot whose name I can consistently recall. I *think*, there-*fore* I-*amb*.

One of my uncles taught me English by misspeaking it. He had been born in the United States but had been sent back to Japan for a proper upbringing. By the time he returned to America as a young man, it was too late: he could not master the language of his native land. Therefore, he and his wife, Tomiko, my mother's sister, conversed in Japanese. She did not call her husband "Fred," as everyone else did, but "At-san." His real name was Atsushi, but that somehow got translated into "Fred." By visiting him and Tomi I learned the startling fact that the world had more than one language. I did not learn Japanese from my uncle, but I learned to pay attention to English because you sounded funny if you spoke it wrong. When my brother and sister and I screamed our way around the house, Uncle Fred would shout, "Too much excite!" When he taught us a better way to catch a baseball, he would say, "Moh easiah." I would cock my head and smile. I could be supercilious long before I had learned the word.

The whole Japanese nation seemed intent on making me mind my language. When I opened a plastic bag of *kakimochi*, rice crackers flavored with soy sauce, I would find therein some moisture-absorbent powder contained in a small paper envelope on which this warning flared: "HARMLESS BUT NOT FOR EAT." Sounding Japanesy—a proper adjective among the third generation in America—was a blunder I had to learn to avoid. My mother told me that when she started school, the other children laughed at her for speaking, with rolled *r*'s, of "grrahhahm crrahkahs."

Since Mom's English had lost its accent by the time she taught it to me, I seldom mispronounced it. However, my mouth got me into trouble in other ways. In first grade I talked too much, or at least at all the wrong times. One day my teacher wrapped Scotch tape around my face like a mummy's bandages, sealing my mouth shut. She sent me home that way, and my mother had to unwrap me.

I learned different lessons from other teachers at school, especially the ones who sometimes strayed from textbooks and lesson plans. My favorite teacher was Mr. Cassel, who was just entering the profession when he taught me in sixth grade. He used to tell of his delinquent youth, when he and his friends would taunt policemen by hollering questions and replies: "What's a penny made of?" *"Copper!"* "What's a peach got on it?" *"Fuzz!"* It was from jokes like this, I suppose, that I discovered the rich ambiguity of language: you could say one thing but mean another. I suspect I had learned that before I reached sixth grade, however.

Mr. Cassel taught all subjects, including biology. One day, in a lesson on the human digestive system, he told us all about the colon. Bernie, one of the smartest kids in the class, raised his hand. He said he had heard of something called the *semi*colon, and he wondered where that was. Poor Bernie. Can he still hear the laughter?

Humiliation, however, is the price of learning. I have never been able to speak a foreign language, and I think it's because I'm too proud. I hate to sound like an ignoramus, uttering the wrong word or botching the pronunciation, but that's what you have to do to learn a new tongue. I, however, hold my tongue and therefore learn nothing. I would rather be an idiot than sound like an ignoramus. Having lost the fearless enthusiasm of an infant, I no longer dare to burble Ah-DAH!

It was in high school that I began to take poetry seriously. I would buy heavy, hard-cover volumes with bundled pages that wouldn't fall out—Collected Poems, paper monuments—by Dylan Thomas, Byron, T. S. Eliot, even Vachel Lindsay. Their words took me to places and times different from my own but also to a state where place and time didn't matter, where everything was merely true.

I memorized Thomas's "Poem on His Birthday," which commemorated his "driftwood thirty-fifth wind turned age." Thomas described himself as "midlife," not knowing he would never see forty, killed by bourbon or by the morphine a physician injected to counteract alcohol poisoning or by, as one of his friends said, being Dylan Thomas; but he inspired me to concoct a long-range plan to mark my own thirty-fifth birthday by ceremoniously reciting the poem. I clung to this plan for eighteen years, occasionally re-reading the poem to keep my memory of it fresh. When the momentous year arrived, I planned that on my birthday, I would drive to a deserted beach and holler the poem into the surf. As the days marched by, I counted down.

But then I forgot. My thirty-fifth birthday came and went, and only several days later did I remember my long-practiced plan. I had forgotten the poem in a way I hadn't anticipated.

Nevertheless, I still call upon Dylan Thomas. Walking on the beach on a bright winter day, I look around, see that I am alone, and commence to intone: "In the mustardseed sun, / By full-tilt river and switchback sea/ Where the cormorants scud . . . ." When I finish that poem, I sometimes segue to Byron, who died even younger than Thomas:

> There is a pleasure in the pathless woods,
> There is a rapture on the lonely shore.
> There is society, where none intrudes,
> By the deep Sea, and Music in its roar.

At last, of course, there is always Prufrock:

> We have lingered in the chambers of the sea
> By sea-girls wreathed with seaweed red and brown
> Till human voices wake us, and we drown.

I studied Thomas for an English class. During my senior year in high school I did an Independent Study in literature, supervised by Mrs. Adams, who had taught me to diagram sentences two years before. She allowed me to read books outside the regular curriculum, ones like *Père Goriot*, *The Divine Comedy*, and *Faust*—all in translation, of course. I read half of *Joseph Andrews*, but then Mrs. Adams said it was too hard for me, so I never learned how that story turned out. When I said I wanted to read Dylan Thomas, Mrs. Adams said she would read him, too. We both loved these lines:

> The rippled seals streak down
> To kill and their own tide daubing blood
> Slides good in the sleek mouth.

When I speak these words, I can feel them warm and slippery and salty on my tongue.

Several years after leaving for college, I heard from my mother that tragedy had befallen Mrs. Adams. Her daughter, who was about my age, had been standing atop an oceanside cliff in Oregon. The Pacific coast is younger than the Atlantic: straighter, taller, more abrupt. The earth collapsed under the girl, and she plunged to her death in the noisy sea.

As a freshman in college, I took three English courses: a required one in composition and two optional ones in literature. In comp I tried to leaven my essays with jokes, but the instructor did not appreciate them. Once she told me my humor was sophomoric. That's pretty good, I said, I'm only a freshman. That's what I mean, she replied without a smile.

For my first paper in literature class I was supposed to analyze a short story by Stephen Crane. I thought the tale preposterous, so I wrote a fictional parody instead of a critical analysis. The instructor said my paper was witty but hard to evaluate because it didn't fulfill the assignment. His system of grading compounded the uncertainty by being difficult to interpret. Instead of letter grades, he gave numbers between one and ten, with one being the best. On the Crane paper I received an eight. "Hopefully," the professor advised me in red ink, "you can exercise your imagination in another way." At the end of the semester, he did some calculations, then announced how the number grades translated into letter grades: a one was an A and a five was a D. That placed my first paper, an eight, somewhere beneath the level of F.

After that, the only way to go was up, and I managed to get a B-minus in that course, the same as in my other two English courses that year. Those three classes accounted for my three lowest grades in college.

During my sophomore year, the college told me I had to declare a major. Several subjects charmed me, but I wasn't devoted to any of them. Therefore, I searched through the university catalogue and listed all the courses that looked interesting—more than a hundred, as it happened. I then calculated whether, if I took every one of those courses, I would have a major in any subject. I discovered that I would be short a couple courses in History and a couple in American Civilization, but I would have enough for a major in English. In other words, I could major in English without taking any courses I didn't want to take. That's how I came to concentrate in the subject in which I had received my lowest grades—by following the path of least resistance.

Ah·DAh!

That has been, in fact, my mode of operation throughout my life. I do not set my sights on a goal, then resolutely do whatever is necessary to achieve it. Instead I avoid opposition and, if possible, seek ease wherever it may be. I do not struggle against the current but let it carry me.

I remember a fable that Chuang Tzu told. He said you should live the way a butcher cuts meat: not hacking against the grain and splintering joints, but slicing smoothly along the natural hollows, so the meat slides effortlessly off the bone. Chuang Tzu did not change the way I lived, but he did teach me how to take the bones off a chicken.

You might say I missed the point, and if you did, you would be describing my entire education. When I took notes at a lecture, I often would get so busy copying the professor's jokes that I would have no time to record the gist of his argument. When I read a novel, I would remember a voice, a metaphor, a phrase, but I would entirely forget the plot. This predilection for the tangential goes back to my childhood. Once I read a story in *Mad* magazine in which this joke was rudely inscribed along the edge of a cartoon panel: "Does your nose run? Do your feet smell? Oh-oh, you're built upside-down." Half a century later I remember the scribbles in the margin but nothing of the story itself. The peripheral is central to me.

As an English major, I read mostly poetry and fiction. I loved Wordsworth, Dickinson, Frost, Yeats, T. S. Eliot, Cervantes, Sterne, Melville, Conrad, Faulkner, Borges, I. B.

Singer, Barth. Perhaps my favorite writer was Joyce: I memorized the long last paragraph of "The Dead." In a book like *Ulysses* every sentence seemed so vivid it could practically stand alone, like a wildflower in a field, its purpose not depending on what lay before or behind. I thought you could open that book to any page, in any order, start reading, and fall in love. I came to despise novels whose principal attraction was their "driving narrative," and I loathed suspense as a cheap resort of the untalented. I loved Shakespeare but mainly for his gorgeous language; I had no interest in drama. When Polonius asked Hamlet what he was reading, the prince snidely replied, "Words, words, words." True enough, but in the journal I began keeping in college, I noted what Shakespeare was writing: WORDS! WORDS! WORDS!

I also loved Nabokov. (Have you noticed how often I say *love*? The word is nearly worn out, but I can't speak of literature without using it.) I enjoyed *Lolita* enough to memorize its first two paragraphs. I noted that when Americans pronounced the author's first name as "VLAD-i-mir," he informed them that the accent belonged on the second syllable—Vlad-EE-mir—to rhyme with *Redeemer*. The job of the writer, I thought, was to take a world that has fallen into meaninglessness and redeem it with the hard gold coins of language. My favorite book by Vladimir the Redeemer was *Pale Fire*, an enormous game. I tracked down the lunar image stolen from *Timon of Athens* ("the moon's an arrant thief, / And her pale fire she snatches from the sun") and the lines emanating from Pope:

Ah-DAH!

> See the blind beggar dance, the cripple sing,
> The sot a hero, lunatic a king.
> The starving chemist in his golden views
> Supremely blest, the poet in his muse.

I thought Pope's *Essay on Man* was an essay on me: a blind, begging, crippled, besotted lunatic blessed by the alchemy of poetry.

I once saw in a storefront window a T-shirt emblazoned with this motto: "life is hard, then you die." That statement was true, I thought; but saying it, finding the words for it, made it cease to be the whole truth. Before you die, you might smile, even laugh—a pyrrhic victory over fate, perhaps, but I'll take any victory I can get. I was going to buy the shirt, but it was black except for the lettering, and I did not want it to serve as a foil for dandruff. Life is hard, but why make it hideous?

I lost my voice in college. In grade school and high school I had been a loudmouth, my hand always in the air except when I blurted answers without being called on. In college, though, I shut up, as if my first grade teacher's Scotch tape were wrapped across my mouth again. In that same freshman literature class in which I boldly submitted an unassigned and impermissible parody of Stephen Crane, I spoke hardly a word out loud, and the instructor gave me a failing grade in "class participation." This public reticence would continue through graduate school, where my silence in seminars and colloquia was duly noted. I would not resume speaking up in class until I became a teacher and muteness was no longer an option.

Why was I struck dumb after high school? In part it was because of my recent discovery that other people sometimes had something worthwhile to say and that I might learn more by listening than by speaking. In addition, however, I went mute because after I did say something, a puzzled silence would often fall upon the group, as if I had missed entirely the drift of the conversation and had introduced a new topic outside the universe of logic. Then, slowly, the talk would resume, picking up at the point just before I had intervened or, if that were not possible, starting with a subject entirely new. I felt like one of those dilapidated men who stand on a street corner downtown and argue with a traffic sign, sometimes kicking it in fury, while passersby turn their eyes away. So, no, I did not want to talk anymore.

What I wanted to do was write. As a sophomore I took a year-long course in Intermediate Writing, in which I produced short stories, essays, poems, and a one-act play. My instructor told me that my natural unit of expression was the sentence but I needed to learn to write paragraphs. He was right and still is.

I live in a universe of fragments. If I told you my life was in a million little pieces, you might think I was just making it up; but I'm not. Is it my fault that things fall apart? If the story of my life looks like a snowdrift instead of a snowman, if it seems like no story at all, it's because it's strictly factual, or at least as factual as memory allows. There's no fiction here, just life. Snow can be lovely if you look at it closely, especially under a magnifying glass. Sometimes you can find the elegance of pattern even in the tiniest events.

In my senior year I supplemented my coursework by attending lectures by a novelist named Jack. For me the best part of the course was to hear Jack read passages of fiction; the words created a world. Once he told the class that there is no such thing as style—there is only voice. Later I told him how much that dictum meant to me, and he said he didn't remember saying it. Jack also has been quoted as saying that "the true enemies of the novel were plot, character, setting and theme" and that "totality of vision or structure" was what mattered. That made sense to me, but he was talking about fiction. I had trouble finding totality of structure in my life.

Even though Jack's course was one in literature, not composition, and I wasn't officially enrolled in it, he agreed to criticize my writing. He read some of my stories and essays and complimented me on them. Then I gave him a batch of poems. When he handed them back to me a couple weeks later, he said, "You know, Jim, I think you have a real gift for prose."

After graduating from college I continued to write: history, journalism, interoffice memoranda. Going against the advice of teachers and the pitiless lessons of experience, I even attempted poetry. After a walk through woods, I composed what I called a haikucycle and named "December":

single snowflakes big as coins
soft as dust twist down
in whitening gyres

obstinate beeches
fists full of dead leaves
shout yellow across the pond

the shrill red maples
made an art form of dying
very Japanese

I liked the shape of the type on the page—the geometry, the architecture. I sent the verses to a literary magazine, but I worried that I had violated the laws of haiku by shuffling the seven-syllable line to different floors of the triple-decker. I was not prepared, however, for the scolding I received. The editor informed me that in a haiku one is not allowed to attribute sentience to mindless objects like trees. I didn't know!

I guess I will *never* know how to write. There must be all kinds of rules that I break all the time, like the periwinkles my boots crumple when I tramp from rock to rock across a beach at low tide. How can I avoid such violations? What can I do? What can I say?

Ah-DAH!

Epilogue

❄ Numbers ❄

Thirty-seven is my favorite number. It is a prime number, evenly divisible only by itself and 1, and this gives it integrity and strength. Its constituent numerals, 3 and 7, are prime numbers, too. Three plus 7 equals 10, the base of our number system. If you add 3 and 7, they disappear down a hole, a 0, with a deceptively potent, skinny little 1 standing beside it. I suppose that not everyone finds these facts as wonderful as I do.

I also love 3, 7, and 37 because they are all odd numbers. Odd numbers are stabler and sturdier than even ones. If you line up thirty-seven objects in a row, the nineteenth will be in the middle with eighteen on either side, calmly symmetrical, balanced like the wings of an airplane. Three is a very strong number. The triangle is the ruggedest shape in geometry; and the pyramids of Egypt, endlessly enduring, have triangular sides, just like the Christian Trinity. The number of cards in a hand of bridge or poker is odd, indicating that the hand is complete. The major American sports—baseball, football, and basketball—all have an odd number of players on the field for each team. Jesus and his disciples formed a team of thirteen. Twelve might have been luckier, but wouldn't it have been awkward at the Last Suppertable to have had six men on one side of Jesus and only five on the other? Every turtle on earth or in the sea has thirteen plates on its shell. A Japanese tea set comes with five cups; a Jewish menorah holds seven candles (nine for Chanukah). The Supreme Court of the United States has nine justices, to avert the inconclusiveness of a tie. Odd numbers are definitive.

Even numbers suggest movement, instability: four seasons and four strong winds, four directions (or six if you look up and down), fifty-two playing cards in a deck, forty-eight for pinochle, the duo Yin and Yang, the sixty-four hexagrams of *The Book of Changes*—changes!—the six lines of each hexagram. There are two teams in an athletic contest, four or sixteen or sixty-four in a tournament. Even numbers are always going somewhere, up or out. When the number becomes odd—1—movement ceases.

I want my age at death to be an odd number. After I'm translated into earth and air, I'd like some rest. I don't expect to be going anywhere.

When I was in high school, I thought I would die at the age of thirty-seven. To a teen-ager, that seemed ripe. Wasn't that the age at which Van Gogh committed suicide? In my books—*Collected Poems of Dylan Thomas* or *Complete Works of William Shakespeare*—I wrote my name not where you might expect it, on the inside cover, frontispiece, or title page, but on page 37. That was my little secret.

As it turned out, however, I did not die at thirty-seven: reality is not as romantic as a boy's imagination. Perhaps I am doomed to a long life, enduring like a pebble of the brook, smoothed and shined by the relentless, chilly rub of time.

It's hard to say when I came closest to death. Was it when I was a baby and the polio virus destroyed my foot but not my lungs? Perhaps it was when, as a child, I got a staphylococcus infection in my skin which, if it had spread to my blood stream, might have killed me. Maybe it was when I, as a youth, was sliding in my sneakers down a glacier on Mount Rainier and almost plunged over a cliff of ice. Then again, it may have been the night I was riding a ferryboat from Newfoundland to Nova Scotia.

I was a young professor on a camping trip with my friend and colleague Clark. Spring semester had just ended, and we—a historian and an archaeologist—were headed home after inspecting the thousand-year-old Viking site at L'Anse aux Meadows. We had found the place covered with snow in June, and we had decided that that was why the Vikings had abandoned Newfoundland. Vikings aren't so tough.

We sailed at night, and although I slouched in a reclining chair, I could not sleep. I walked out onto the empty deck and, as usual, positioned myself at the bow, facing the cold wind. I stood at the railing and looked down at the churning black water far below. I thought about its vast depth and endless extension beyond any horizon, any possible succor. You can drown in a pond or stream. You can drown in a bathtub if you really try. But the ocean is different: it's *made* for drowning. I thought it would be easy to climb the railing and go over. My body would never be found—"unknelled, uncoffin'd and unknown."

I wondered whether I would actually die by drowning or whether I would first succumb to freezing in the icy North Atlantic. Or would it be, after a long plunge through the unresisting air, the sudden concussion on the hard surface of the sea? I wondered if my falling body would even reach the water before being batted away like a volleyball by the onrushing hull of the ship. Would I be flung to the side, bobbing momentarily in the waves, or immediately sucked down into the gigantic triangular hole the prow was gashing into the sea? I could not perform the calculations of ballistics and hydraulics needed to predict my fate.

You might wonder whether something was bothering me. Not that I recall. I had suffered no disaster or even any particular disappointment recently. Everything was normal. It's not that I wanted to die; just that at that moment I had no objection to extinction.

When I stood at the ship's railing, looking straight down at the sea, I had a familiar feeling: the dread of heights. Most people have a fear of heights that is rational. They know a cliff is dangerous, so they make themselves stay away from the edge and watch their step. For me, though, the fear is not rational, but physical: a feeling unlike any other, an upwelling chill in my groin—not in

Numbers

my sexually definitive organ but just beneath it, near where I suppose my prostate to reside. A numbness seeps through the rest of my body, leaving as my only sensation an amorphous, stony coldness deep in my viscera. It is not pain but extreme discomfort, as if my soul were emitting a silent but incessant scream. My eyes pull me toward the rim of the cliff, while my torso leans stiffly away. I want to drop to the firm, sustaining earth and wriggle on my belly to safety. I want to curl into a tight ball and shut my eyes. I want to be somewhere else, I want that intensely, and I want it instantly. Of course, there is only one way to do it instantly. All it would take is one little step.

What is dread but fear inflamed by desire?

What I need to banish dread is a sturdy wall: the steel fence around the observation deck of a skyscraper, say, or even the chest-high railing around the basket of a hot-air balloon. As long as a physical barrier makes it hard for me to jump—how unseemly it would be to climb over!—then I have no desire to do so and therefore nothing to fear. But that night at the ship's railing, I thought of climbing.

My cowardice saved me, as usual. As I imagined a tumble overboard, I thought of the painful chill of the water on my skin, the cold penetrating my limbs, and the discomfort of gulping the salty sea into my lungs. What if, as I plummeted through the air, I suddenly found that I had changed my mind? Would not that discovery be an unhappy one? Better to play it safe, I decided. So I went back into the main cabin where Clark and the other passengers were sleeping, and I spent the rest of that long night shifting restlessly in a chair. What saved me, then,

225

was not so much my will to live as my aversion to the unpleasantness of dying.

A few years later Clark told me he was getting married, and he asked me to be his Best Man. For the wedding I flew to Johnstown, Pennsylvania, site of one historic fatal flood and two later ones that were ordinary catastrophes, easily forgotten. There I met Clark's bride, Christine, her parents, and her ten siblings—it was to be a Catholic ceremony.

One of Chris's sisters lived in Andover, Massachusetts, only a hundred miles from me, on the other side of Boston. Observing how she fit into her family, I noticed that she was like a second mother, looking after everyone. When she found out that Chris had a sore throat, she volunteered to drive to the supermarket for cough drops. She took me with her. She realized that I was an outsider, never having met anyone in either family but the groom. To keep me from being isolated in a crowd of strangers, she made a point of involving me. Later we sat in her parents' living room, and—inevitably, since I was involved—the conversation turned to food. We talked about Italian restaurants in Boston. She had a favorite one in the North End, and I had one near the Common. We decided to get together and try them both after we got home.

The sister's name was Barbara.

I was thirty-seven.

A NOTE ON THE AUTHOR

J. A. Hijiya was born in Spokane, Washington, in 1949. He was educated in the public schools (Washington Irving Elementary, Lewis and Clark High) and at the public library. From the age of twelve to the age of twenty he worked for the Spokane *Spokesman-Review* as a paperboy, copy boy, reporter, and copy editor. He majored in English at Brown University, then switched to History for his Ph.D. at Cornell. He taught for two years at Ithaca College, then twenty-five at the University of Massachusetts Dartmouth. He published two academic biographies and a dozen scholarly articles, as well as occasional feature stories and op-ed pieces in newspapers. After retiring from teaching, he wrote this volume of personal essays. He wrote Chapter Four before the implantation of artificial lenses transformed his eyes from extremely near-sighted to somewhat far-sighted, making his vision almost normal.